She Went Ahead

A Mother' ~

G000144379

Ruth Gatting

www.apostolos-publishing.com

First Published in Great Britain in 2018

Faithbuilders, An Imprint of Apostolos Publishing Ltd,

3rd Floor, 207 Regent Street,

London W1B 3HH

www.apostolos-publishing.com

British Library Cataloguing-in-Publication Data

A catalogue record for this book is available from the British Library

ISBN: 978-1-912120-536

Cover Design by Spiffing Covers | spiffingcovers.com

Printed and bound in Great Britain by Marston Book Services Limited, Oxfordshire.

Nicola Joy

A little flower, lent not given,

To bud on earth but bloom in heaven.

Acknowledgements

First of all I give thanks to God, whom I believe commissioned me to write this book and inspired the writing throughout. There were times of pain, as I relived the worst memories, but also times of joy as words seemed to fall into place. I'm thankful for all those who walked with me and were such an encouragement to keep going!

A special thank you to my amazing husband, Dave, who has been alongside me the whole time, spurring me on, giving me hugs when it got too much, with prayer and practical advice. Also to my wonderful sons, Steve and Paul, who read my story, gave comments, reminded me of things I'd forgotten and who are so supportive about me sharing our family story with the world!

Thanks to my dear friends, Lillias Chawner and Judy Neale, who put me in touch with Laura Treneer, Chief Executive at Christian Publishing and Outreach, who pointed me to Apostolos Publishing. Thank you, Laura, for all your encouragement and practical help. Sadly Lillias died unexpectedly before the book went to print and is now in heaven herself. Her husband, David Chawner, who was chairman of Ealing Cruse Bereavement when I was a counsellor and supervisor with them, checked through my manuscript and gave valuable input. Thank you, David, and God be with you as you now walk through the grief journey.

Thank you Sue Rugg, for doing some vital tidying up of my manuscript prior to it going to the publisher, saving me some embarrassment with my bad punctuation! Thanks to all my friends who have prayed for me through the two years of writing. I thank especially my long term friend, Ros Hardwick, who walked with me through the journey of grief, has believed in me and encouraged me with writing the book and still blesses me with her friendship. Thank you Chris Curtis, my special friend who has also prayerfully supported me through the writing of this book.

Indeed, thank you to all those who came alongside us as a family when Niki died, too many to name but you all played a vital part in our healing and restoration.

Finally, a big thank you to Mathew Bartlett, my editor, for all his hard work and patience with all my questions, what a blessing!

Contents

1

Our Family

"Come on Mum, it'll be great! Don't be scared!"

The children were so excited! It was June 1987, and we were on holiday in The Black Forest, Germany, and at this moment we were at the top of a big hill, at the start of a dry toboggan run. It felt like a mountain to me – it looked a long way down. I'm not so good with heights or slides, and was hanging back as Steve (12), Niki (9), and Paul (5) were spending their precious pocket money to go careering down the hill. It looked safe, don't get me wrong, as it was a proper metal run, and the toboggan had a brake – which I intended to be in control of! Well, I didn't want to be left on my own as they all disappeared at speed!

I climbed into a toboggan with my daughter Niki; my husband Dave got on with Paul, and Steve was allowed to go on his own. What a ride, it was amazing! I noticed a sign on the bends – "Langsamer!" – a new German word for us, telling us to slow down. I quite agreed! We all loved it, and so we started walking again, up the hill, to do it all over again. I think we were saving money by not going up in the chair lift as we did the first time. This time I went down with Paul, feeling more confident that I could cope without Niki's help. All their remaining pocket money went on that ride.

The Black Forest was a beautiful place to be, with hill upon hill of dark evergreen trees, and rich green valleys dotted with traditional timbered farmhouses and grazing cows. It was a quiet peaceful place with rivers and lakes, picturesque villages, and small towns. Freiburg, near to our campsite, was an attractive city with ornate old buildings, especially its cathedral, as well as lovely little cafés.

The campsite where we were staying was great for the children, with plenty of other families there. Niki was the confident, outgoing one, who led the way in making friends, her brothers following on. She was not afraid to go to the shop and use her little knowledge of German to buy milk and bread each day. If there was a hill to walk up, Niki would take the lead, up front ahead of the rest of us, or perhaps with her Dad, the only one who could keep up with her. Sometimes the two of them were the only ones who got to the top, as I had to look after Paul with his little legs (that was my excuse anyway!) and Steve would play the big son and look after me.

We were a very contented family, with Niki the extrovert, and Steve and Paul more introvert like their Mum and Dad. Steve was two-and-a-half when Niki was born, and was her protector, often seen sitting with her – the big brother looking after his toddler sister. When Paul was born, Niki was nearly four, and she loved having a baby brother. Once she started school and was learning to read, she would sit with Paul and read to him and try to teach him to read. As she got older, if there were babies around, Niki would be playing with them, or carrying a baby around on her hip. She had a natural mothering instinct.

Steve and Paul were also good with small children, but if Niki was there they found it hard to get a look in. Close friends of ours had twin baby girls whom our children loved, and with two to play with there was more chance for Steve and Paul to join in. Niki was often the leader, and could be bossy with her brothers, but she adapted to playing with each of them differently and was definitely the link between them as the middle child. I loved our family.

I had always wanted three children, coming from a family with just one brother, much older than me. It felt perfect. I was very content, though it was hard work at times, of course, as they had their fair share of fights and arguments, and I'd hear the cry, "Mum, tell him!" or "Mum, tell her!" When Dave came home from work I'd think, "Great, now he can take charge," but often it was still me that had to sort out the rows, when Dave was sitting with the paper or watching TV, relaxing after work. He was quite oblivious to what was going on around him at times!

I wrote this poem when Paul was two years old, Steve and Niki being at school:

Mum's Prayer

Dear Lord, I feel so battered
And bruised at the end of this day.
It's not so much my body
(Though that is aching — you know)
But my mind that feels so tired,
My very soul, and spirit, worn out.

The morning went well, I suppose,
Though busy — I was in control;
I even remembered You, Lord,
Once or twice, I thank you for that.

Two men were mending the gutter
And putting slates back on the roof,
So lunch was rather disrupted
By "Scuse Missus, got a bucket?"
And "Thanks for the cup of tea!"

But they did it well, as you know,
And for a reasonable price;
I can see your hand in that, Lord,
In a very "down to earth" way!

The afternoon disappeared —
I suppose it always does;
With the trip to school and back
The family was doubled - to four.
Why should that make so much difference
To the level of noise at home?

In addition to "Mum, wipe my nose!"
And cries of "Potty!" all day,
It's now "Stop it!" "Don't!" "Go away!"
"Mum, what's for dinner today?"
"I'm hungry, Mum, what can I eat?"
"Mum, can we watch telly now?"

And in between the answers
I attempt to cook a meal
(And gather in the washing
And mop up a spilt drink or two!)
Now at last it's ready
Won't they be glad to eat?

But what are these cries I hear?
"Do I have to wash my hands?"
"Lay the table? I always do it!"
My programme's not finished yet —
I'll come in a minute, ok?"

At last we sit down to eat,
(Was it worth the effort, I ask?)
"Look out, your hair's in your dinner!"
"Cut that meat, first!" "Mind your drink!"
"You get the sauce if you want it!"
"Lean over, that shirt was clean on!"

Oh good, that sounds like Dad's home,
Some relief for me at last;
No, it's still "Mum" this, "Mum" that!
Oh why don't you ask your Dad?

But what would I do without them?
I long for some peace and quiet,
Yet when they're all out and I have that
I'm happy for a while — say an hour —
Then I long for them all to be back!

Yes, I thank you, Lord, for my family,
For the turmoil as well as the peace;
Because it's all part of the jigsaw
That you're making of my life, of me!
And every piece that is fitted
Brings me nearer to completion — and you!

So what was Niki like, the middle child of the family? She was confident, outgoing, and always wanted to be doing something, whether it was out on her bike or roller skates, with friends, playing a game with Steve, playing pretend games with Paul, reading, drawing or writing. She was good at school, and loved learning, and getting good marks for her work. She loved writing, and wrote very neatly in her school books, something her brothers never quite achieved!

She made up a code once and wrote me a message, which she had to translate for me of course. It read:

"I know why you look so buitiful all the time mum, because you get it off your children (me of chorse). To you from Nicola."

It showed her cheeky sense of humour as a child, and her not so good spelling!

Another one was to Steven, her big brother, showing what she thought of him in spite of all the fights:

"You are super star of super stars. To Steven from Nicola"

Ah, sweet!

Although we all called her Niki – except me when she had been naughty, then it was NICOLA – she always signed herself Nicola. I can't find anything signed as Niki, and am not sure now how we came to spell it that way, as it's not the way most people would spell it. I guess we just wanted to be different, like the girl herself. The meaning of the name Nicola, from the Greek, is 'victory' and 'people', implying the meaning 'a winner of the people', and she was like that – popular with her peers and always wanting to win in competitions. She was a leader, adventurous, outgoing, and impulsive.

She would draw pictures for me, like one of a boat after we'd had a riverboat ride. She wrote on it:

"To Mum, this is the boat we went on today. You are at the back saying be careful. I love you, from Nicola".

Yes, I was definitely the one saying be careful, hanging on to my daughter as she leant over the side. She was the one most likely to have mishaps and accidents.

For example, in one of her school exercises she wrote of a holiday we had in Cornwall, where we stayed in a bungalow, with my parents staying in the bungalow next door:

"One day we went to a place called Bodbin. [It should be Bodmin!] In the car park there was a duck pond, we gave the ducks some bread. There was a baby duck there, I tried to throw it some bread but it was too far away and I fell in. I was lucky because we had just been to the laundrette so I had something to wear. But they were damp. My granddad, my mum and I went to get me some more wellington boots to wear because I was wearing leather boots. When we got back my granddad kindly washed and dried my boots for me."

This did not faze us – it was typical of Niki! All in all, there was never a dull moment when Niki was around.

2

Family Ups and Downs

1986 didn't start well. Steve and Niki both used inhalers, as they suffered from asthma, and more recently, Paul had also started having breathing problems. He had to take medication in the form of syrup to help at such times. At the end of January, he had a very bad asthma attack. He was only four-and-a-half when he was taken ill in the night. We gave him the syrup, but he was vomiting so it was not having any effect. Dave was always reluctant to call a doctor or ambulance, wanting to make sure it was absolutely necessary, but this time we nearly left it too late. I think it was a lesson for Dave.

Paul was taken into hospital at 7:30 a.m. and put on oxygen, with a drip too. He was quite scared, poor mite, but eventually calmed down. Niki and I were there with him all day, and then I stayed the night with him. Thankfully by the morning he was able to sit up and enjoy his breakfast, a good sign. He had to stay all day that Saturday, while tempers frayed in the family, until finally he was released about 6:00 p.m. We all had a good night's sleep that night.

Towards the end of the year, I was in A&E again with Paul, when he had a tight chest and breathing problems. This time I had taken him in as soon as there were signs, and we were both more relaxed and back home again by 8:00 p.m. Better safe than sorry, that's my motto!

Not to be outdone by Paul getting all the attention, a month later Niki broke her left arm during the lunchtime break at school. Because of her asthma, she had to stay the night in hospital after having it set, so they could keep a check on her. It was a difficult time for us both, as I stayed with her overnight, but she was allowed home by 6:00 p.m. the next day. We'd just started having central heating installed, so there was a massive clean-up that day to avoid any trace of dust setting off an asthma attack.

Christmas was looming again … what presents to get for everyone? I had a brainwave for our parents: we'd have a family photo done, the five of us, and give one to my parents and one to Dave's mother, and keep one for ourselves, of course. We had never done that before, unbelievably, so it seemed an inspired idea. We found a good photographer and got on well at his studio. It was quite a formal photo, typical of the time, with Dave and the boys sitting and Niki and I behind. Niki had her head on her Dad's shoulder, snuggling up. She was always like that, a little girl who loved cuddles. Dave called her his little princess, and they had a special bond. The photos were received with pleasure, and one went up on our wall too.

As the year 1987 began, I continued keeping a journal, something I had done on and off for a year or two. I started it because I wanted to write down how I was feeling and what God showed me as I read the Bible. I'd been a Christian most of my life, and was brought up to have a time on my own each day – to read my Bible and pray. Although this is a good discipline, it can become just a routine, and with three children it was not easy to do every day anyway, especially when they were small.

I was feeling at the beginning of 1987 that I was a bit dry and stale spiritually, needing refreshing. I resolved to try harder to have these times alone with God, wanting to be like a boat in a lock in a canal – shut away from the world for a while, waiting to be lifted up to a higher level, ready then to sail out on the next part of the journey. I kept coming back to the words "Find rest, O my soul, in God alone."[1]

On THURSDAY JANUARY 8th I wrote:

> To be able to walk closely with God I have to start by resting in God, because that involves complete trust on the way, the path I am going to take. I can't choose that path; I take the steps … God directs the path.

These quiet times soon hit difficulty, as in the middle of January the school was closed because of frozen pipes. The children were home for a week, and just before the school opened again Steve went down with flu, then Niki caught it, so I had no chance to be alone for a while!

A month later I found myself writing a poem, something I'd been doing from time to time over the last few years. I would get the first words in my mind and as I wrote them down, the rest flowed. This time it came out of frustration – I was telling God how I felt and asking what purpose he had for my life. Then he started answering me, as had happened before.

Frustrated - or Floating?

Oh Father, I'm so frustrated,
I can't see what you're making of me;
I don't know where I'm going,
The way ahead I just can't see.
You've said I need a vision
Or else I will shrivel and die.

I've had such beautiful glimpses
Of what you want to do through me;
But that's all they are - just glimpses,
Flashes lighting up the night sky.
Why don't they stay, Lord, and grow
Into days of beauty and light?

Now together as a couple we stand,
Taking knocks of frustration daily, all round;
We're propping each other up, just about,
But what if we both fall down?
Lord, if we're both weak together,
Who's going to help us get up?

In the midst of people we're alone,
Seeing no hands to guide us as one.
There are those to support me, Lord,
Close friends to help me along,
But who strong enough to support us both,
And together to lead us through?

Where are you in all this, Lord?
Our eyes are searching all round;
Getting frustrated with people, with people,
Battling, struggling, fuming or just despairing,
When will our lives ever bear fruit?

Well you two, look at you ---
No wonder you're always so tired!
What about resting - remember?
"My soul, find rest in God alone"?

You sing "River, wash over me",
But you're thrashing wildly about
Like a child just learning to swim.
If only you'd lie still you would float!

But Lord, if I'm going to float
I've got to lie flat on my back.
That's a very vulnerable position -
I won't be able to see where I'm going.
No, I'd much rather be swimming, Lord,
With a definite goal in view.

Yes, swimming is good, my children,
You find satisfaction, reach goals;
You think floating around on your back
Is so aimless, frustrating and cold.

But there are times when I need you to float,
Then you have to look up to my face;
I've got to know that you'll trust me
When you can't see the way ahead.

Just remember - when you're floating
You're renewing your strength for the swim,
And it's vital that you learn deep trust
For the journey you're about to begin.

While you're floating, you _can_ trust me,
You've every reason to rest:
I'm above you, to see the way ahead,
And I'm the water holding you up!

I thought it was a wonderful picture of God's care for me. I'd just read this verse in the Bible: "Then we will no longer be infants, tossed back and forth by the waves."[2]

I longed to find that sort of rest in God, with Him seeing the way ahead and also holding me up.

When I shared this poem with Dave, he was concerned about the lines: "It's vital that you learn deep trust for the journey you're about to begin." It seemed like God was preparing us to go through a hard time. Dave thought something bad was going to happen to one of the children, but I didn't want to think about that, and eventually it went out of our minds.

I wrote in my journal at the time:

> "Thank you, Father, for giving me such a lovely family, and the home to make for them. In all this, I thank you for your love, for the caring things you do ... for the children's natural appreciation of your place in the home. I lift you up, Lord, in the centre of this home and family, to be worshipped and adored. I love you because you're you, and you're always here with me; and yet in your magnificent way you are far above everything. With that panoramic view, you lead me in the best way, yet you are right with me, holding me up, comforting and reassuring me in your arms."

A few weeks later I started feeling ill, so ill I could not get out of bed. I had laryngitis, lost my voice, and felt very sorry for myself. I remember Dave making a recorded announcement for me to hold to the phone if it rang: "Ruth has lost her voice and cannot speak to you, but don't hang up. Please leave a message for her." It didn't work very well, people were quite confused, and usually hung up! It was unusual for me to be this ill. Furthermore, the antibiotics made me nauseous and sick, worse than ever.

Just as I was beginning to feel better, a strike began at the children's school and they had to be kept at home. I did not cope well with the next four weeks. The children eventually went back to school, three days before breaking up for Easter!

Don't get me wrong – I loved my children, and really enjoyed spending time with them, but I also needed time out for myself and when I was not able to have that I could get quite impatient and grumpy. God was teaching me lots this year – about myself, about walking with him … but I had no idea how things were going to change for us, devastatingly so.

WEDNESDAY MAY 20th

We set off for a special family holiday – we had to be at Dover for 9:00 a.m. Gosh! How did we get there at that hour? It was fun right from the start, the children loved the ferry across to Calais. From there we drove to Luxembourg, where we stayed for a few days with a family that used to live next door to us.

We left Luxembourg a few days later and started our drive down to the Black Forest, Southern Germany. The story cassettes we took along helped occupy the children during the long drive, and so did the travel games, but it eventually got a bit boring and there were the usual cries of "Are we nearly there?"

Finally we arrived! It was wonderful – a beautiful camp site at Kirchzarten, near Freiburg, with mountains all around. What a great place for the children, miles away from the London noise and traffic. They quickly began to make themselves at home on the campsite, exploring and making some friends.

We soon discovered the swimming pool next to the campsite, and the children loved sliding down the chute into the water. It was such good weather too. We enjoyed exploring the area with its mountains, and even drove into Switzerland one day. We had fun at a theme park, as well as doing some mountain walks, but the highlight was definitely the toboggan run that I described earlier.

The only down side was Niki feeling unwell towards the end of our time there, with a sore throat. Yet it didn't stop her climbing right to the top of a church steeple in Freiburg. She loved being up high - the opposite to me with my nervousness of heights.

I remember we visited a couple whose daughter was connected with a friend of ours back in England. When she heard we were going to the Black Forest area she said we must go and visit her parents. We were a bit nervous, taking three lively children to visit a German couple that we'd never met. As it happened, Niki was not lively as she was feeling unwell, but she kept going and helped the boys to fit in and play with the toys and games provided. After a lovely afternoon tea, and sociable time, we were thinking of leaving, when suddenly we were told we were staying for dinner. The German hospitality was amazing!

Well, after a wonderful holiday with lots of fun together as a family in the fresh air and beautiful countryside of the Black Forest it was time to pack up, and start the long journey home.

Little did we know what we were going home to. Thank God we didn't.

3

Back Home: The Nightmare

TUESDAY JUNE 2nd

We left the camp to travel back to Luxembourg, to stay with our friends again for one night, and then on to Calais for the ferry home. Looking now at a photo of the children on the ferry I can see Niki was still not herself, sitting quiet and pale on the deck.

We arrived home late on Wednesday evening.

THURSDAY JUNE 4th

The children had missed a few days of school (no threats of fines in those days!) so after letting them sleep in and rest for the morning, we took them back to school after lunch.

That evening we had a parents' evening with the teachers to hear how they were doing. I remember Niki's form teacher telling us how bright Niki was, how she was usually the first to put her hand up to answer a question and she had to be encouraged to give the rest of the class a chance to catch up! She'd written a great imaginative story, I remember, about going into a land in her desk, like Narnia.

FRIDAY JUNE 5th

Dave had the day off work, to finish off his holiday, and we were looking forward to our day together.

We spent the morning talking and praying together. We were feeling unsettled somehow, still frustrated as in the poem, not knowing how God wanted to use us. What was our purpose? He seemed to remind us that he is our Rock in every situation.

As we read a Psalm from the Bible, I remember these words being impressed on us: "The Lord is my rock ... in whom I take refuge.... The cords of death entangled me.... In my distress I called to the Lord; I cried to my God for help. From his temple he heard my voice; my cry came before him, into his ears."[3]

From my journal that day:

> Dave asks God for a definite sign about our immediate future.

That was unusual, not something we had done before, and I cannot remember ever doing it since.

At 1:00 p.m., the phone rang ... it was a call from the school. Niki had fallen over and they thought she might have broken her arm. Thinking of how she had broken her left arm the year before, we thought "oh no, not again." We were in the middle of our lunch, but we went immediately to the school. I was so glad Dave was with me this time.

Niki was very distressed that she'd probably broken her arm again, especially as this time it was her right arm; she hated getting behind with her school work.

> In Casualty, I was very distressed too – that she had to go through all that pain and discomfort again, maybe miss her school holiday and the dance show coming up.

> 3:00 p.m. – I leave to fetch the boys from school. By the time I've brought them home, got Paul to Lucy's, it's about 5:00 p.m. when I reach hospital and the children's ward where Niki is just being settled into bed.

Lucy was Paul's best friend at nursery, a sweet little girl with lovely parents, so we got on well as families, and often helped each other out with child care for the two of them.

> She went to theatre about 7:00 p.m. so we came home to see Steve, and grab a bit of tea. Dave went to a leaders' meeting at church and I went back to wait for Niki, about 8:30 p.m. Glad it was short plaster (not round elbow) and no drip. Worst over now, and Dave's staying the night with her.

She was admitted for the night as before because of her asthma – to keep an eye on her breathing after the anaesthetic. That was okay, we'd done this before.

Niki able to suck ice cubes. Paul at Lucy's for night –
strange just Steve and me at home. Had good sleep.

SATURDAY JUNE 6th

Dave rang – Niki had restless night, found it hard to
sleep with arm up, and still in pain, not wanting any
food, just orange juice.

I fetched Paul about 9:20 a.m. and we all went in to see
Niki. Dave took Steve and Paul to sports club at 10:00
a.m., and came back about 1:30 p.m. after MacDonald's
lunch. I went off for lonely lunch at MacDonald's.

Niki's arm and fingers beginning to swell – plaster split
right down to try and relieve pressure, still up in air.
Could move fingers then. I'm prepared to stay the night
– hope of Niki coming home is going fast. Temperature
still keeps shooting up.

This was not alright anymore, she should have been feeling
better by now. What's going on?

Some years later, Paul wrote in a school essay what he was
feeling at this time, as a five-year-old, nearly six. At first it was
just annoyance, that Niki wouldn't be home and he would be
bored, as she looked after him so well. But as the day went on
he began to worry, seeing Niki with her arm suspended, not
being able to talk to him, and the serious faces of the family
making him uneasy. This didn't happen last time Niki broke
her arm, he thought. She should be home by now ….

About 7:00 p.m. I took boys home ... had tea, got Paul
to bed, and then back to hospital for night. Niki dozing
quite a bit of the time but when awake is not very
happy, still in lot of pain.

As she has ward to herself, I have mattress on floor near
Niki – much better. Didn't get it till nearly 11:00 p.m.
as only 2 nurses on – too busy.

Every time I tried to sleep, Niki wanted a drink. Once I
got a bit cross and she managed to sit up and get it
herself – I felt so guilty, or do now. She got more and

more unhappy, more and more difficult to comfort, yet I didn't know what to do as often only one nurse around and so busy with babies.

Eventually I plucked up courage to fetch a nurse, and when she saw how hard and swollen Niki's arm was above the plaster she called the doctor. He eased the plaster right down and put ice packs along it. Didn't seem to help Niki much.

SUNDAY JUNE 7th

5:30 a.m. I rang Dave in desperation, I was so upset at Niki's agony. He came in to the hospital. More painkillers and icepacks, which help for a while.

About 7:00 a.m. I went home. Breakfast and back to hospital so Dave could go back for breakfast then take boys to church (they were happy there with friends, in their classes). Dave joined me again, Niki sleeping more now, we thought it good for her to rest, and a doctor told us to let her rest, and not fuss over her.

By this time the tension was building up … I had that awful feeling in the pit of my stomach. It's so desperately hard seeing your child in pain, and not being able to do anything about it. I longed for the doctors to do something, anything, to make her better.

I left about 12 noon to pop home, then fetch boys from church — I got weepy there, Niki having such a rough time. Plan to leave boys at H's (friends' house) after lunch — for couple of hours. Left them there about 2:30 p.m. and back to Dave and Niki. Niki's temperature still up and down, and Niki having more delirium (as last night, everything seems far away to her).

She kept thinking we were at the end of the room, when we were right by her bed. It was scary, not knowing what was happening to her. My close friend Ros, who had the twin baby daughters, was very supportive.

Ros came for couple of hours — helped me sew name tags on Steve's clothes for his computer camp tomorrow. Still having to bathe Niki's forehead. Ros fetched boys for us then went home.

About 4:00 p.m. Doctors all round Niki — took plaster right off and arm up higher then swelling should start going down. But nil by mouth in case surgery required — Niki keeps saying she NEEDS a drink — my heart is breaking.

I can't bear this ... Lord, DO SOMETHING...

Then they come to take more x-rays — her poor arm is so swollen — fingers puffy but still pink, bruising round her wrist and elbow. It's agony for her while they get her in the right positions for x-rays, I can hardly bear it, poor love.

When left in peace she dozes quite a bit, but is getting more and more delirious — not talking any sense, and reaching out with her left arm at things that aren't there.

Next time the doctors see her they look really worried — now when they touch her hand it stays white for a while. I know it's not good. Her arm looks terrible now.

She's prepared for surgery — they explain that they will slit down her arm to relieve pressure (I worry about the awful scar) and they hope that will enable the blood to get through to her hand again.

I take boys home after Dave and I see her up to theatre — she looks so frightened, her eyes wild. Oh God, I love her so much — please get her through this soon. Told Dave to ring when she comes back, and went to sleep about midnight.

1:50 a.m. Phone rang — worst moment of my life ... Dave says Niki is in ICU — things not good. They tried for 3 and ½ hours to get blood through to her hand, but pulse only at elbow, not wrist.

When the surgeons had opened up her arm to try to relieve the pressure it was like cottage cheese inside, with a huge infection, which had grown in the site of internal bleeding in her arm. At some point, they had started pumping her with antibiotics, but ...

Dave said it looks as if Niki will lose her arm.

I screamed "Oh God NO!" Dave asked if I was ok and I said I didn't feel too good now.

The sickening pain inside me was overwhelming.

I can still recall the heart wrenching fear ... please God, NOOOOO!

4

Indescribable Pain and Fear

Dave came home and we cried together. We read Psalm 18 and prayed, and after about an hour of praying, crying, and talking I was calmer, even with the awful sickening feeling still there. We both had remarkable peace when Dave went back. He hadn't been able to see Niki but was going back to wait in ICU. I couldn't get back to sleep, until an hour or so before alarm went.

I had a picture (A vision? A dream? I don't know if I was awake or asleep) of Jesus carrying Niki up a hill (it was like a silhouette in the distance). I thought that meant she would be ok, even though it would be an uphill struggle.

I said to God that we'd cope with Niki losing an arm as long as she had an experience with Jesus while she's asleep, so that she could feel him close. Please God, that's my prayer.

I started thinking how I'd work with Niki to learn how to use my left arm along with her. But I kept thinking of things she wouldn't be able to do with one arm … she'd hate it. I made a vow that as Niki would have to learn to write with her left hand, so would I. We would do it together. We loved doing things together – shopping, having a drink in a café, walking together, she always wanted to hold my hand or take my arm when we were out. We could get through this together.

But it was still awful, she would be devastated when she found out she'd lost her right arm, absolutely devastated. She was so active; how would she cope? Would she shout and scream? Yes, she would. The last time my dad had seen her she was having a tantrum about washing the dishes! She was definitely one to show her feelings.

MONDAY JUNE 8th

Steve packed and ready for holiday, but I felt absolutely terrible. Dave rang before we left for school, and whilst on the phone the surgeon came urgently for permission to remove Niki's arm, a desperate attempt to stop the infection from going to her brain ... to save her life. They were waiting for a brain scan, as Niki hadn't come round after last op, and they thought she'd had movement down right side, but not left.

9:00 a.m. Niki is in theatre.... Dave came home to come to school with me – Steve had to be there by 9:30 a.m. Paul was a bit late getting to his class, and his teachers were horrified when we told them the state of things. I also told H and A (friends) but trying not to let Steve see how bad things are. I was agonising over - were we doing the right thing sending him off? It was a nightmare doing that, knowing that Niki was having her arm removed, and was critically ill, absolute nightmare. I can't describe the awful feeling in my whole body. Steve looked worried – I felt guilty for sending him off in ignorance. He knew she was in ICU and wondered why.

The doctors had advised us to let him go, hoping that by the end of the week Niki would be improving. How we saw him off, I don't know. It was so hard seeing him go. As my journal entry shows, I felt so guilty, sending him off not knowing how bad his little sister was. He'd always looked after her, kept an eye on her at school too. After the coach had departed, we told the other parents and teachers, and they all cried with us.

We went home then. Our friends, Chris and Ros, came round at our request. Chris was a nurse himself, so was probably very aware of what was going on with Niki. We had coffee together and prayed, then they came with us to ICU. Niki had not regained consciousness. I could only stay there with her for a few minutes, it was awful ... I thought I'd pass out.

She had gauze over her eyes as they wouldn't shut properly, and would dry out, so they put drops in. she had a tube in her mouth for respirator but apart from that, and a urine bag, her body was functioning. Body temperature was a bit low so they put a foil sheet over her till it came back to normal. Lots of tears with Ros.

Next time I saw Niki I was able to stay for longer, and sit and hold her hand and talk to her.... Perhaps she could still hear.... The consultant came to see us, with the doctor who told me "Don't fuss, mother." He can't speak, he is so upset. The consultant explained how the inner skin (fascia) can't stretch, and had swelled up with slow bleeding from the fracture going into muscle cavities, so much that blood can't get through — tiny arteries damaged by this pressure. He also explained that Niki's brain was swollen, and she was being given a whole range of antibiotics to get rid of the infection that was in her blood.

Had rung Mum and Dad this morning so hoping they'd be up at home soon. Dave popped home and I stayed. Chris and Ros left but Ros came back with crisps and apple (all I wanted for lunch).

Two other close friends came in. They didn't see Niki, which was for family only at this point, but it was such a help having their company in the waiting room for a while.

We saw Dr Silverman that afternoon.... Niki didn't seem to be responding and he seemed to be talking about turning off the machine if there was no positive result from tests tomorrow morning. I panicked — said you can't just turn off the machine, you've got to leave it longer. Can't remember what he said, but it was no comfort. (Dave thinks he said there was a critical moment for Niki when they nearly lost her — in the morning?)

I felt dreadful coming home — cried with Mum, then with Dad. We didn't eat properly. We felt desperate —

arranged to meet with church leaders for prayer. Went back to see Niki briefly, talked to her, hoping she could hear us ... but she couldn't respond. I'd asked them to cover up where her right arm should be ... I wasn't ready to cope with that yet. At one point the ventilator went wrong and they had to use a hand one while they got a new one set up. It really frightened me – the man doing it really erratically – doing other things at the same time.

This is my daughter! You must keep her alive!

She was still being pumped with antibiotics, but she was showing no signs of responding. It was becoming more and more likely that Niki was not going to make it ... we were losing her ... I was filled with utter grief, desperate ... there is no way to describe it.

We met with our church leaders, who prayed with us, and cried with us too.

Prayer for wholeness and health for Niki – nothing less. B. prayed for me as a mother. He said God was crying with me as a mother ... God has a mother's heart as well as a father's. We left with peace, hope for Niki restored I believe, to give us a good night's sleep.

We'd thought about staying at the hospital, but felt we needed a good night's sleep and if we had stayed it would have been in the little room they gave Dave the previous night - some way from where Niki was, so no point. Either way they would ring if there was any change.

That evening the rest of the church had met and they were praying too. Ros had a picture of Dave and I leaning against a rock (must be Jesus) with the rest of the church in a circle, linking hands, facing towards us. Eileen had a picture of Niki on Jesus' lap.

TUESDAY JUNE 9th

Woke about 4:00 a.m. (both of us) – talked about bringing Steve back home, donating organs of Niki's if *she didn't make it. Asked John (Lucy's Dad) to take us in to hospital — couldn't face hassle of parking. Talked to Dr Silverman — didn't give us much hope, but tests late morning. He said we should think about getting Steve home and facing this as a family, or boys might feel left out later. Went to see headmaster about 12 noon. He rang through to the camp; we decided a teacher would bring Steve home by train. He rang to tell us train times. We went back to the hospital with cassettes to play to Niki.*

(Another friend, a nurse herself, had lent us a Walkman and suggested we play Niki her favourite music ... she might still be able to hear.)

The anaesthetist (Jane) attending Niki was very kind and helpful, and she took the time to explain to us Niki's condition.

She told us Niki's heart rate was high, and increasing, and blood pressure fluctuating. She said Niki's brain was partly dead, the part that controls heart rate, and that even if Niki regained consciousness, she'd never be able to do anything for herself, not even breathing. Niki as we knew her, had gone. She was getting pale now, and seemed under stress. We broached the subject of organ donation. We were fairly calm — it seems amazing now, but it was God's grace and strength, completely.

Jane helped us to see that Niki was so far gone that she would never be the same again. In fact, she would never even be able to breathe on her own again. It was the beginning of our saying goodbye to her. We were beginning to let her go ... to heaven, where she would have a new body.

Jane also encouraged us to bring the boys in. We went to Euston to fetch Steve. We were in quite a state of tension ... and early. Glad to see him, but when we got to the car, and Dave started to talk, he burst into tears so I took over, until I too couldn't talk. Between us, we explained to Steve how things were, and he cried with us then.

We drove home more calmly, even picking up a neighbour we saw on the way and telling her about what was happening to Niki. At home we sat down with Paul … how do you tell a five-year-old that his big sister is going to die? It breaks your heart….

He sobbed and sobbed. In his own words, he wrote later: "I cried and cried for a long time, it was as if I was stuck." He couldn't believe that Niki was not going to survive.

We took the boys, my mum and dad, and Elizabeth (Dave's sister) to see Niki. We warned Steve and Paul about all the tubes and breathing apparatus but – as it had been for me at first – it was all too much for them. They didn't want to go close to Niki. They didn't like it, with the machines whirring and clunking, and their sister, motionless.

> Steve was very upset. Back in the waiting room, he sobbed and said "Niki, please don't die … keep trying, Nik". Oh, my heart's breaking….

I have to say, the doctors and nurses were wonderful, on the whole, and they were distraught for us. They had not seen anything like this before, a patient dying after breaking an arm. The surgeon felt it, he told us, as he had a daughter about Niki's age. We kept in touch with the nursing sister for some years afterwards; it felt like a link to Niki, I think.

> Nurses had washed Niki's hair and tied it up with white tape – she looked like a beautiful young teenager. I've been heartbroken that I wouldn't see her grow up into a young lady – now it's as if God's given me a glimpse of her grown up, to ease the pain. She looks so beautiful, and a bit more restful.

> Dave and I saw Dr Silverman and the donation lady. More tests tomorrow morning (legality) to finalise brain death, and machine off then, as long as we are at peace.

Other friends and family came in to see Niki. A meal brought over by a neighbour was much appreciated. Cooking was something none of us could think of doing, but we needed to eat, to keep our strength up.

At this point I had a phone call from a friend of a friend who had been through the death of her daughter. It helped a bit to listen to someone who had been through it, and survived.

WEDNESDAY JUNE 10th

> I woke up very early again. Kept boys home today. Mum and Dad are going home today, coming back tomorrow.

They said they wanted to vote in the election. They had been amazingly strong the last couple of days, a big support for us as a family, but probably needed time away, to let themselves feel their own grief, before coming back into our desperately sad situation.

> Paul gone to Lucy's for the day — they'll bring him back later — and they're cooking us a meal and staying the night, we've been told!

More family came over to see Niki early that morning, so Dave and Mum went to meet them at the hospital. They came back after but didn't stay long as Andi, my niece, had an A-level exam that afternoon, poor girl.

> Dave, Dad, and I went in then, to see Niki; Steve and Paul didn't want to go, but Ros came (wants to see Niki). We didn't realise that anyone can go in to see her; I always assumed it was just family. She is very upset too. As soon as I saw Niki I said, "Gosh, she looks so peaceful today." The stress was gone, her cheeks were pink again. When Jane came in, she said exactly the same thing to me. I said "She's not there — she's already in heaven." It helped me in saying goodbye, but I still found it hard to leave. I kept kissing Niki and crying — Jane and another nurse there too — wished I could have been on my own, but didn't like to ask.

> It was just a formality to see Dr Silverman, to hear the results of the tests. No brain activity. Talking about organ removal. At last minute, we hear her heart is needed, not just kidneys. This really helps us to cope

with Niki's death. But they must be removed before the machine is switched off — that is hard.

One of Niki's kidneys was given to a 3-year-old child and the other to a 22-year-old girl, and her heart was given to a 50-year-old-woman — she must have had a new lease of life, I thought! I wish we could have met these people ... it wasn't possible in those days. It did help to know that in her death Niki brought life to three other people. Something good had come out of it already.

We're trying to wait for my brother who is supposed to be on his way, but Dad finds out he's been delayed, so we can't wait. Niki's heart could give up at any moment — the longer they wait, the less chance they can use her heart. So we gave them permission, and were just leaving when M. (a friend) rushed in. She was expecting to see us at home at lunchtime, and we were late so she'd rushed down to the hospital. I was so glad she got there — I wanted her to see Niki, so I took her in to say goodbye. She came back with us then, in our car - I was so glad to have her support.

The strength was suddenly draining from me and I sat weakly on the sofa. She cried with me, arms all round me.

She had been wanting to give her support but even friends at a time like this are not sure when to visit. I had asked Dave to ring her this morning and ask her to come round, so she felt that was her answer, and was really glad of the opportunity to show her love and try to give some support.

When she'd gone I went to bed — I feel so weak and washed out now. The tension's been so great, but now I can let go, or start letting go. My brother arrived while I was in bed. We're going back when hospital rings (after op) with Niki's clothes.

The mother who rang me, who had lost a daughter, gave me this thought, as they had encouraged their other daughter — who had been away when her sister died and found it hard to accept – to see her afterwards, when she was dressed in her favourite clothes and jewellery.

I didn't sleep but my strength returned. When I came down my brother hugged me like he'd never let me go, and cried and cried. We had not seen each other for some time, after his divorce and remarriage.

Dave and I, my dad and my brother went to see Niki's body after the organ donation. We gave Steve and Paul the option, but they didn't want to go, and Mum stayed with them. They couldn't take any more. We took Niki's lemon jogging suit, which she loved wearing, and a ribbon for her hair.

Niki looked beautiful, in her own clothes, and the nurses had done her hair as I'd told them she liked it, and put a flower in her hand, but Niki was gone … she wasn't there.

5

Emptiness

THURSDAY JUNE 11th

Today is a rest day, recovering from all the tension, or trying to. We feel very weak, but almost relieved in a way, that it has ended. The tension of the last six days has been enormous, we realise now.

The tension, the dread and the anxiety had been all-consuming, and we were absolutely shattered. The fight was over. We had no strength left. We were going through the motions of living, within a vacuum....

Friends poured in throughout the day. It was election day, and the children were off school because the school was being used as a polling station.

One of my friends went off to ASDA with Steve to do the shopping. Steve was the practical one and knew exactly what we needed. He also needed the time out, a distraction from the trauma and grief.

Paul had his friend Lucy round for company while her mum acted as our bodyguard so that we weren't bothered by anything or anyone who might be unhelpful at this time.

Mum and Dad were back that afternoon.

Our kind neighbour brought another meal.

The phone never stops ringing, but Dave and I don't answer it yet. Dad is marvellous at that, and Mum is coping amazingly with all the cups of tea.

They too were devastated, but I think it helped them to be able to do something useful.

We were managing to get some sleep at night, we were so exhausted, but we usually woke about 4:00 a.m., when it all hit us afresh – Niki had died. The brutal reality came crashing in, overwhelming us again, like a tidal wave. I can't put into words the pain and distress of that fresh realisation every morning.

FRIDAY JUNE 12th

The coroner rang, and we went back to the hospital. We saw Dr Silverman, the consultant paediatrician. We were trying to find out why Niki died. There was no more from the post mortem yet; just that she had a swollen brain and an infection in her bloodstream. It was all a mystery, even to the doctors.

We had to start sorting out practicalities ready for Niki's funeral. I couldn't call it a funeral, though; funerals are for old people, I felt. I insisted we called it Niki's farewell service.

My Dad helped us as we went to the funeral directors, and the florists, to choose flowers for wreaths. It was so hard making these decisions, we wanted it to be just right.

We were going through the motions, doing what we needed to do, like zombies, emotionless.

The enormity of the huge crater now in our family didn't bear thinking about … it was too much.

There are no words to describe the emptiness.

6

Our Support Network

It was all a bit surreal, and looking back, I wonder how we coped with all the things we needed to organise, but I know we were carried by God, and felt the effect of all the prayers being made for us.

We couldn't have coped this far without our wonderful support network.

Letters of condolence began pouring in. It was a source of comfort to us, to know that so many people cared, and were thinking of us and praying.

As friends and neighbours came to visit and offer their condolences, they often didn't know what to say. This was in a letter from a friend who came round soon after Niki died:

Although I was really looking forward to being with you both and I really wanted to see you, I was anxious about what to say/do/how to act ... I thought I might make things worse for you as I felt so sad and devastated about Niki. But I had a lovely time with you. People keep asking me how it went and they don't seem to be able to grasp that it could be such a time of blessing. I came home feeling that I'd been really ministered to.

Ruth, when we were on the phone and you told me about Wednesday evening at your home and the 'amazing atmosphere' there, I thought how can that be? But on Thursday I experienced it for myself. God's love was so present with us in the situation. There was such a feeling of healing at your home and I felt, and continue to feel, so much at peace. It was so good to be talking about Niki — how she was, and what she is doing now, having a great time with the babies in heaven. And it was just lovely to see you and how despite everything, you were okay.

One neighbour who came to the door started crying as Dave opened the door, he had no words. So Dave just gave him a hug! That was our message to people who didn't know what to say – just say nothing, just give us a hug – or a touch, to show you care. That's all we need.

There really are no words.

They worried about making it worse for us. How could anyone make it worse than it was? Yet, as people testified, God was carrying us in a way we had never experienced before, such that people were blessed as they came to see us. They were amazed at the strength we seemed to have.

It's hard to describe the mixture of emotions in those first days. There was relief at first, as I said, after such immense tension; there was grief, usually coming out when we were on our own. Then there was appreciation of the support and comfort from so many lovely people, which brought joy amid the sadness. It often takes a tragedy to see how much people care about you, and how they then grieve with you, and for you.

Looking back, I realise how much I depended on my friend Ros in those first months of grieving. So often I would cry on her, and then apologise for not being good company. She would tell me to stop apologising, that she didn't expect anything of me. She was grieving too because she loved Niki, but she was still able to be a comfort to me. Although she was in our lives so much through this, she wrote down her thoughts in a letter to me:

> Because written words are so precious to read and read again and to treasure in our hearts when times get difficult.

How true that is, as I read them again, three decades later.

She continued:

> Words cannot adequately express the deep sorrow that has come upon me. These last few days have changed my life in that God has flooded my life with his love and especially for you. I loved you before but I love you more deeply now, because it's not just my own natural

love but it is God's love too – and it's too immense to comprehend or try to describe. I feel that because you have lost a part of you that a part of me has gone as well.

She went on to assure me that our suffering is not in vain, and that God will use it for his purposes and glory. Someone else wrote: "I am sure that one day the Lord will use this terrible bereavement that he has trusted you to bear as a means of blessing others."

That is something that was on my heart from the time it happened – to use our experience for good to help others; but more about that later. I hope and trust that is also now happening as you read this book.

Another friend wrote that God had increased her love for us as a family through all this. It seemed that God was pouring out his love for us like a waterfall, and pouring it through people around us, so that we could feel it in a physical way too.

Letters from people who knew Niki were of particular comfort to us, especially when they wrote lovely things about her:

- We will always cherish the memory of a wonderful and lively girl who came often into our house to play ... who was so full of all those things that we see and love in bright and vibrant children.
- Such a happy young girl dashing around on her roller skates.
- I shall always see her with a little girl in her arms ... she had such a wonderful 'little motherly' love for all the babies in the church.
- Niki was a lovely little girl – I can still see her playing snowballs in our garden last year.
- I will always remember Niki. To me, she was one of the cheekiest girls but with a heart of love.

From the school doctor:

We will always remember her as a lovely, sweet and kind girl. The clinic staff join me in conveying to you our heartfelt condolences.

Some of her school friends at the time were clearly encouraged by their teachers to write down their thoughts and memories for us. I'm sure this helped them, as well as being a special blessing to us.

- I've wrote this letter for you about Nicola when she was a monitor with me to do the TV. I can remember when we were monitors. She had to go first all the time because I was scared because the doors kept creaking. We used to love to do the job because we got the chairs first. Once I lost the video key and I looked and looked … in the end Nicola found it.
- I am in the same class as Nicola, and I am very sorry about what happened to my friend. I liked and loved her very much as my friend and I feel very, very sad but I will always think of her and the fun we had.
- Nicola was a good pupil and she was good. She hardly needed help. She was a good friend and she believed in God.
- Nicola sat next to me and when I would start to do my work she would put an arm on my desk … and even helped me do my work.
- I would like to have a photograph of Nicola (*they all wanted one*) because she was very kind and helpful to me and it will be very nice to look at.
- I liked Nicola very much and she was a very good friend of mine.
- Nicola was very funny. Once she put her ruler under her plaster of Paris and she said, "Look, my ruler has gone through my hand!" [*That was the first time that Niki broke her arm.*] I liked Nicola a lot.

From the chair of governors at the school:

Nicola's life in the community that is our school has had an influence which we will all remember.

If there *were* any words we wanted to hear, it would be that Niki would be remembered, that her life would not be forgotten. As I have met parents or teachers years later it has been really uplifting to hear that they have not forgotten Niki.

7

First Few Days as a Shattered Family

SATURDAY JUNE 13th

We went, with my parents and Dave's sister, to our friends, Chris and Ros for lunch. Their twin daughters were about a year old, and Niki had so enjoyed looking after them. She loved babies and small children, and was often seen with a baby or toddler in her arms. It was a lovely atmosphere there, with gentle music on as we sat round the table to eat.

After lunch, Dave, the boys, and I dashed off to meet my niece, Debi, at a circus that was performing locally. Debi's boyfriend was one of the clowns, and they'd got us tickets to try to help us, bless them. We were finding that we couldn't bear to be alone, just the four of us now – Dave, myself and the boys. Is that how we describe our family now?

I think we enjoyed the show, as a bit of a break, until I saw a girl with a ponytail, in a yellow jogging suit like Niki's. Oh Lord, I can't bear this…! But we shared it as a family, we were all in this together, this awful journey of grief.

Paul, our youngest son, seemed to be coping best so far, after the initial tears. We were warned by the paediatrician that at his age, nearly six, he would react as it affected him. That was such an apt and wise warning, as on the ride back from the hospital on the last visit to Niki, Paul was sitting in the back with Steve and said, "There'll be more room in the back of the car now!" Ouch! That hurt so much, but we couldn't blame him. That's how it was for him.

Then within days, he was asking if he could move into Niki's bedroom! He had been sharing bunk beds with his big brother Steve, and Niki had the small room to herself. Now Paul saw that he could have that, which honestly turned out to be a good thing, after the initial shock. Niki's room was not going to be left empty or untouched like a shrine. It would be occupied by a small boy who loved his sister. It did stay pink for some time though, with lots of Niki's things in there. That could not be changed quickly, but instead bit by bit, as I could cope with it.

Paul had a lovely understanding of Niki in heaven. It was so real to him. He had a very natural way of talking about her as still part of the family, like the way he talked about sharing her bed with her now. She had been a wonderful big sister to him, teaching him to read, and playing games with him. I recently discovered a cassette tape which Niki must have recorded. She was playing with a friend and Paul, and they were reading jokes and stories to each other. As they took turns to read, it came to Paul's turn and there was a whisper from Niki telling him what to say. He was probably not old enough to read it all so she prompted him – that's what she was like.

She could go from playing pretend games with Paul – like mums and dads, or shop and customer – to playing board games with Steve; as long as she was winning! If Steve was winning, she often got bored and gave up, much to Steve's frustration. Without Niki, there was a huge gap between the boys. They weren't used to playing together without Niki. She was the go-between, the one who blended the children together. Without her, they were lost, as we were.

The pain of losing a daughter I had carried within me for nine months, given birth to, cared for, nourished, always been there for, scolded, disciplined, but always loved with all my heart, was indescribable.

When I gave birth to my firstborn, I was surprised to have a son, I thought it would be a girl. We didn't have the option of knowing beforehand in 1975. I guess it was something to do with my dolls always being girls. I couldn't imagine looking after a boy, but it was a wonderful surprise, to have a firstborn son. I felt so proud to have given Dave a son; it was very special.

But when it came to deliver my second baby in October 1977, I was really wanting a girl. When she was born, it was a moment of utter joy! I kept asking the midwives, "Are you sure? It is a girl?" It felt like a completeness somehow, I had a girl in the family. I thought of all the things we could do together. It was wonderful!

When I was expecting my third child, I sensed it was a boy, and we should call him Paul. I think it was God telling me. Paul was born very quickly so it was quite traumatic. Suddenly he was there – Paul Jonathan! I was very happy, having my one daughter now to have two sons. The family was complete, and each addition had been excitedly received by the older siblings.

Now in the course of just one week, our beautiful family had gone from perfect to utterly broken, shattered. It was like an explosion had occurred and left a huge empty crater in what was once a beautiful place. Our family unit was destroyed for ever. It would never be right again. How could we go on? For me personally, losing Niki was like having part of me brutally ripped out.

SUNDAY JUNE 14th

Just four days after Niki's death, we were with our church, and it was like an extended family around us, loving us. I told them about the poem "Floating" I had written earlier in the year … it had dawned on us now that God had indeed been preparing us for something terrible. I also said it felt like a beautiful vase had been broken, but it would let out a fragrant perfume. Something wonderful had to come out of this sacrifice to make it worth the pain. Some friends there had us round for the rest of the day – there was a lot of love pouring over us.

MONDAY JUNE 15th

I woke at 5:00 a.m., going through the farewell service and burial. Having seen myself throw the soil on the coffin I felt a dreadful finality – there was nothing else to do for Niki now, and the vacuum was all consuming. Dr Silverman had warned of this; he gave such helpful, practical counsel. I was feeling a foretaste of that vacuum. Yet there was so much to do, so many people to tell, it all seemed too much. Dave and I were trying to contact everyone in our address books to tell them what had happened, and about Niki's farewell service. So we got a letter typed and printed about a hundred copies to send out. Dave also went back to work for a short day, to try and break himself in again; it was so hard for him.

I went back to the florists with my parents so that they could order their flowers. I was having doubts about the colour of our wreath, and wanted to change it. It was so hard to make decisions in the numb state I was in. Eventually I decided on a cushion of pink and white flowers.

TUESDAY JUNE 16th

My parents went home for the day. I think they needed to get away for a break in some way, as well as checking mail, etc. After the boys had gone to school, Dave and I spent some time together, talking and praying about Niki's farewell service. When Dave left in the late morning for work, I was on my own for the first time, so I went to see Ros. Dave and I found that we both needed to talk about what had happened and how we were feeling, our fears, worries and so on, and Ros was the one who was always there for me. Our friendship went deeper as I shared my grief with her and she shared her twin daughters with me. With two babies, it was good to have two pairs of hands and we could have one each to look after. No one could replace Niki, but it helped to have another little girl in my arms at times to love and care for.

I went to the school on my own for the first time to meet Steve and Paul, my dad having been there with me up to now. But he was one step ahead of me, as he and my mum had come back in time for him to meet me at the school. What wonderful parents! More of the mums at school were approaching me, wanting to show they cared. They all felt it so much – it could have been their child that had died. Some of them would cry with me, which was hard for Paul, upsetting him at times. He didn't really want to let us out of his sight, but he would happily go to his friend Lucy's house and her parents were a great help to us still.

Letters and cards kept arriving, thick and fast, as friends and family received our sad news. It was really kind, but hard at the same time. It made it even more real. The amazing thing was that whilst on our holiday in Germany, Niki had posed on her own several times. As the photos arrived, it was bittersweet: they were so lovely, and yet she wasn't here anymore. We had lots of reprints of these photos done so that we could give them away – something else to keep me occupied, with my dad's help.

Sometimes I was alone, or just with my parents, and I felt low and lost, and then the doorbell would ring. It was another friend coming to keep us company. God seemed to send people just when we needed them – always a step ahead of us, just as he had been in providing all the photos.

Niki had been in a dance class which was due to have its first performance just weeks after she died. That was really hard. I'd made all the costumes and they were hanging around the house. Her teacher, Pet, rang me, saying such lovely things about Niki that I couldn't stop crying. She said that Niki still had her place in the show, as if she was still there – no one was pushing her out as if she didn't exist. They didn't fill Niki's place in the show, they just left a space where she would have been.

I wrote at the time:

Everyone is so lovely, it overwhelms us.

Going back to the registrar, who told me not to fuss over Niki when she was in such agony and delirium ... I guess he remembered what he had said to me, as a week later we received something in the post from him. It was a bookmark from St. Paul's Cathedral, and on the back he had written these words, from the Bible:

> Every test that you have experienced is the kind that normally comes to people. But God keeps his promise, and he will not allow you to be tested beyond your power to remain firm; at the time you are put to the test he will give you the strength to endure it, and so provide you with a way out.[4]

I don't remember how I felt on receiving that. Not much I think, but I can see now the truth of those words. I saw it as his way of saying he cared about what had happened to us, so I don't want to think badly of him for the way he spoke to me. I'm sure he learnt from this experience that even doctors need to listen to the mothers of the children they are treating.

8

Saying Goodbye

FRIDAY JUNE 19th

There was a lovely little service at the school for Niki, with children from her year, parents, and some teachers. It was a special thing to do, the headmaster was really caring, and so many cried with us.

Sunday would be Fathers' Day – not good timing. I took Steve and Paul to get cards and chocolates for their Dad. How he would miss his little princess.

MONDAY JUNE 22nd

Niki's farewell service. There had been some trepidation about the Press being there as it was such an unusual death, and enquiries by the Press had been made at the hospital. As it happened, this was not a problem, and the report of Niki's death did not get into the local paper until after the inquest.

I woke after a disturbed night, feeling terrible butterflies and a sickening feeling. How would I get through this day, especially being the centre of attention with my grief? How would Steve and Paul cope?

I feel better now I'm up, though the waiting is awful. Flowers are arriving. I feel calm in spirit, if not in body. Sun was shining earlier, but a bit cloudy now. Hope it doesn't rain. Paul has chosen a few roses from the garden to put on Niki's coffin, bless him.

That's something a child should never have to do; it seemed so wrong. I was so proud of our lovely sons and how they were coping with all that was happening.

It was hard to wait until 11:00 a.m. My brother arrived; it was good to see him again.

By the time we left for the service, it was drizzling with rain, which continued all day, reflecting our mood.

The church was not large. It was packed. There was standing room only in the rear half, as everyone struggled to fit in. There were children and parents from the school; the school had closed for the morning. There were also children from Niki's dance class, with her lovely teacher.

The service was beautiful. Steve, Paul, and I all were all crying. Dave coped wonderfully, speaking about Niki and sharing some lovely memories of her. I remember him telling about our recent holiday and how Niki had insisted on ordering – in German – her own food at McDonalds in Freiburg. We could still picture her walking back to the table with her tray, and a big smile on her face! Dave kept it together while he shared these precious memories. Later in the service, when one of the other speakers choked up with emotion, Dave became tearful too.

There was lots of music, as Niki loved music. We'd chosen the hymn, "The Lord's my Shepherd," feeling that truth for ourselves and for Niki, as I had seen that vision of Jesus carrying her up the hill, like a shepherd carrying a lamb close to his heart. We also sang "Ascribe Greatness to our God, the Rock," remembering that God had impressed that on us the morning that Niki had her accident – he is the Rock in whom we take refuge.

We played two songs from a cassette that Niki loved singing along with. She was actually one of the voices on it as it was a recording of a children's group at a Christian camp we attended as a family.

> Love goes on, it will always be
> Deep and strong, like the mighty sea
> You don't know how long his love goes on.
>
> Love goes on, it will always be
> Deep and strong, like the mighty sea
> You don't know how long his love goes on.
>
> I often do wrong, but his love goes on,
> I'm sorry 'cos I've hurt him, but his love goes on.
> He loves to forgive, but his love goes on,
> His love goes on...

And another:

> Jesus wants to take away your sadness
> And pour on you the oil of his gladness
> Jesus wants to fill you with his goodness
> And turn your worry into praise.
>
> So give him all of your cares
> Because he cares for you
> Give him all of your life
> And let him give his life to you
>
> So give him all of your love
> And let him pour his love on you
> Because he cares, he cares for you
> He cares for you.

It was as if Niki was singing to us in our grief.

We finished with this song, which a lady from our church had written in a card to us, reminding us that Jesus had carried Niki into heaven, one of the jewels in his crown.

> When he cometh, when he cometh
> To make up his jewels
> All his jewels, precious jewels
> His loved and his own.
>
> Like the stars of the morning
> His bright crown adorning
> They shall shine in their beauty
> Bright gems for his crown.
>
> He will gather, he will gather
> The gems for his kingdom
> All the pure ones, all the bright ones
> His loved and his own.
>
> Little children, little children
> Who love their Redeemer
> Are the jewels, precious jewels
> His loved and his own.

Afterwards, I stood outside under an umbrella and tried to prepare myself for all the people who would come and speak to me. Ros, bless her, was the first one to give me a hug, and to be there to give me support.

Niki was being buried in my home village in Berkshire, about 25 miles away. When we had to start thinking about Niki's funeral, cremation was out of the question as far as I was concerned. No way could I have her beautiful little body burned; but the cemeteries around us in London were such grim places. We often passed the one nearest to us on our way out in the car, and I remembered Niki saying as we drove past, "That's a sad place," and so it was: grey tombstones surrounded by industrial buildings. No, we couldn't lay her to rest there.

However, in rural Berkshire where I had been brought up, and where my parents still lived, there was a lovely little cemetery just a mile or so from my parents' home at the end of the village, and just along the road from their small church. It was up a small lane and surrounded by trees and green fields. Two of my uncles were buried there and my parents expected to be buried there too. So, my dad, bless him, got in touch with the local authorities and bought a plot for Niki and one for him and my mum at the same time so that they would be near each other.

This was a place where I could come and mourn, remember Niki, and be at peace in a beautiful quiet place which was well kept with flowers and trees all around. At times, there is a horse in the next field, or a glimpse of a deer. The deer eat the flowers though, so I have learnt over the years that it is best to put silk flowers on the grave as the deer don't seem to have an appetite for those! Last time I was there, a young fox met me in the lane and led me into the cemetery, disappearing as I got my phone out to take a photo.

After Niki's farewell service, we made the long slow drive down there with the cortege. It was really encouraging to find so many had made the journey with us, including several of the teachers from Niki's school. What caring people all around us!

We were concerned about Paul seeing the burial as he was so young to go through that, seeing his sister's coffin lowered into the ground. So we left him at my parent's church in the care of my sister-in-law. (It was only much later that he told us he was upset at the time, as he felt left out. It's so hard in grief to know the right thing to do, or the best thing at the time. Perhaps we didn't explain it carefully enough to him?)

The burial was utter anguish – the coffin bearing my daughter being lowered into the ground ... there are no words to describe the pain. I can't let her go! This should never be happening, putting my child into the ground. So final, so harsh, so devastatingly terrible.

And then, to make it worse, when we went back afterwards to see all the flowers, we found that the undertakers had buried with Niki the lovely wreath we had chosen.

We took so long to choose that wreath; it was a beautiful pink and white cushion of flowers. It was to be on the grave with the other flowers, with all the cards, as is usually done. Now it was buried, out of sight, and I was absolutely gutted. It was like rubbing salt in the wound, my lovely last gift to Niki was buried in the earth.

They meant well, I suppose, the undertakers. But I'm sure they never asked my permission. I was absolutely devastated. It seemed such a stupid thing to do. I went back to the Funeral Directors and complained, but with no energy left to fight I had an identical wreath made, and within days I travelled the twenty-five miles back to the cemetery to lay it on the grave with the other flowers. Even in grief I was determined to get things right for Niki.

It felt like she was missing out on so much – not only her first dance show, she had also been due to go on her first school trip away the following week. She was so excited about these things, and now she was no longer here. They would all be happening just the same, but without Niki.

In fact, everything else was going on the same, but Niki was gone. I remember going to the supermarket for the first time after her funeral. It was so hard seeing things I would buy for her, but now there was no need. I felt so empty, and heavy hearted. Everyone else was going about their business as usual, but I couldn't. Everything was going on just the same, but it seemed so wrong. How could life just go on the same? I felt like shouting – "My daughter has died!" I was an empty shell, feeling I would crumple into a heap at any moment. Why wasn't everyone crying with me? It sounds silly, but that's how I felt.

Grief is not logical and it's not predictable either.

During this period of utter, black emptiness, I wrote this poem:

Life without Niki

Last week we buried our daughter.
How cold those words are to my ear.
Oh God, the pain, the emptiness
Is more than I am able to bear.

Every way I turn Niki's there –
Her photo, her drawings, her toys;
So much of Niki around me,
Surely she must walk in soon.

She always liked to be near me,
She'd walk hand in hand, or hold my arm.
Oh God, my arms are aching
To hold her, and keep her from harm.

Today I opened her dance bag,
And there were her dancing shoes still,
We were so looking forward to the show,
To see her dancing on stage – what a thrill!

I was going to make her hair pretty;
The costumes I worked on so hard
Just enhanced her beauty – Oh God,
Why did she have to die?

The school journey was drawing near,
Her first holiday away from home.
She'd planned which cuddly toy to take,
But five days before ... she died.

Oh Father, the hurt is so bad,
As if part of me has been wrenched out.
Do you understand what I mean?
Do you **really** know how I feel?

I bore my daughter, I loved her,
I looked after her just nine or so years,
I scolded, I corrected, but I loved,
So much love, now so many tears.

People mistook us for sisters,
A compliment I took that to be!
But that's how it was beginning to feel
As she grew up — such company for me.

She broke her arm, infection set in,
And as much as the doctors tried,
They could not save her arm,
And five days later she died.

I don't know how she'd have coped
With no right arm to use.
I know there'd have been lots of tears
As together we tried to adjust.

But now she's in heaven with Jesus,
With a body that's new and whole;
And the show that she's in right now?
So spectacular — it cannot be told!

She's dancing before God's throne,
In shining, glimmering white!
Her eyes are sparkling like jewels,
Her beauty — a wonderful sight!

She's in the middle of it all –
Just as she liked to be here –
Loving the little children and babies,
A special helper for Jesus there.

Thank you, Lord, that she's with you,
You heard my prayer as she slept
In that coma, so peaceful she looked,
That close to you she'd be kept.

Now Father help us to forget
The pain and the suffering she bore.
Give us the peace and joy Niki's found,
And heal our wounds, Lord, so sore.

God's answer to me

I watched my Son die, remember?
I could have saved Him from that;
But then you couldn't have been my child,
And Niki wouldn't be with me now.

I felt the pain that you're feeling,
And I'm feeling it now with you.
But as you share in my suffering,
So you'll share in my healing, too.

I will heal your wounds, I will,
Because I delight in you,
The love, joy, and peace that I give
Far outweigh all the grief that you bear.

The joy that will come in the morning
Is far greater than you can imagine;
So keep trusting, and rest in my arms,
And let me work out the way.

It helped me to write down my feelings, and I felt – as in this poem – God was listening to me as I wrote, and spoke into my mind what he wanted to say to me. It was like a warm glow came over me, and for a while I had peace in my heart – until the next trigger.

9

The Journey of Grief Begins

WEDNESDAY JUNE 24th

Midsummer's day, and the school put on an afternoon of dance, each class playing their part. Paul was great, a big grin on his face as he danced, concentrating so hard, but enjoying it so much. Then it was the turn of Niki's class. I found myself scanning the faces for Niki, hoping it was all a bad dream, a mistake, and she was there after all. But she wasn't.

A friend came back with her children for tea. How we appreciated the distraction when good friends and family came round, knowing that they were sharing our grief. They didn't try to say things to make it better; they just spent time with us. They knew how much we needed company.

I must say here, the support we received was amazing, and the letters and cards kept flooding in. Some came from people we didn't know directly, but they had heard from a mutual contact and wanted to tell us how much they felt for us. I've just read them all, as I write this, and there were about one hundred and thirty-five, plus another ten or so from Niki's friends. We were grateful for them all, but the best ones were the ones that spoke about Niki in some way – about what a beautiful girl she was, so lively and full of fun, and cheeky at times too!

When I see how many of the senders said they were praying for us, it's no surprise that we experienced strength in the depths of our grief. This was especially so in that first week or two.

I received a letter in the post from one of Niki's teachers. He had been at the farewell service, and was writing to us later that day with his memories of Niki. He wrote:

> My contact with Nicola in the 1st year at school was through science, and she was always one of the more perceptive and knowledgeable pupils that I had the pleasure of teaching. She always seemed to exude a

> sense of maturity and confidence beyond her years and in fact our mutual sense of fun led to Nicola having a special form of address, one that I used with great affection and one that always caused hilarity with Nicola – namely "the honourable Miss Gatting!"

How thoughtful to tell us those little memories. That's the sort of letter that warms the heart of the bereaved. He also said that during the school journey the week before, wherever they were their thoughts were all with Niki. One afternoon, whilst taking a group around Brownsea Island in the sunshine, among the pines, rhododendrons, peacocks, and rabbits, they stopped. With the blue sky above them, they prayed and thought of Nicola. He said those few moments would stay with him for a long time.

What a treasure of a letter, making me cry, yes, but to know that Niki was being remembered like that was very special.

FRIDAY JUNE 26th

We went to stay with friends for the weekend, a much-needed break when we didn't have to do anything except eat and sleep. The couple we were staying with did not have children of their own, but were really good with Steve and Paul. Another family joined us on Saturday and in the huge garden much fun was had with the motorised grass cutter you could sit on. There was also an opportunity to play on a miniature golf course. It was generally relaxing after the intense days of stress and tension.

SUNDAY JUNE 28th

Reading Psalm 23 this morning – new depth of meaning for me now – "Even though I walk through the valley of the shadow of death I will fear no evil, for you are with me; your rod and your staff they comfort me."[5] How? The rod beats off the enemy, and the staff picks me up when I fall over, or catches hold of me before I go over a cliff. Thank you, Lord that you won't let me fall prey to the enemy, or black depression; you will restore my soul. Although the path goes through the *dark valley now, you won't leave us there — you're going to lead us out to a green, spacious place. We can't imagine how, that's why we've got to trust you completely.*

MONDAY JUNE 29th

We left our friends and had a day out at Whipsnade Zoo on the way home. We'd had such comfort with friends looking after us for a few days, giving Steve and Paul some fun, and just being there with us. Then we were suddenly on our own, the four of us again, and it was so, so hard. I kept feeling guilty for being there without Niki, as if we'd sneaked off without telling her, especially when we went on the train round the zoo. Niki had always wanted to do that, but because we usually had the car there it was not necessary. This time we didn't take the car in.

Then we went into the café and Dave was looking round for a table for five, his heart broken again. Will we ever get used to being just four of us? We don't want to! With all our hearts, we don't want to! There's such a gap, such an emptiness; it's a physical ache in our gut.

We got home to more mail, letters that made us cry because they were so lovely. I found there were raspberries ripe in the garden and had just started picking them when in walked my mum and dad. They thought they'd welcome us home, but we got there first. What a lovely surprise! They came laden with delicious fruit for our tea. What thoughtful loving parents, driving for forty-five minutes to be with us for a few hours, realising it would be a hard day for us.

It's good in times like this, when everything looks so black, to thank God for the things that help, the people who show they care, the little things that light up our world for a while.

There's a Psalm which says: "What joy for those whose strength comes from the Lord…. When they walk through the Valley of Weeping it will become a place of refreshing springs. The autumn rains will clothe it with blessings. They will continue to grow stronger."[6]

It's true – when we have to rely on God for our strength, he does not let us down. Just when we need some help he provides it.

TUESDAY JUNE 30th

The first morning home, and after breakfast Paul was crying with toothache, saying, "Take the pain away, Daddy." Dave's heart was breaking; how sensitive he was now to anything that upset the children. Some medicine helped and we got a dentist's appointment in the afternoon. That was another hurdle, to tell the dentist that Niki had died, and to take her off their records. I just about got through that and made a hasty exit before I broke down. There were other things like that – informing the GP, stopping child benefit, telling people I met in the street, or the shops.

We could only live from day to day. Each day's tasks seemed like mountains to climb, things that before were just molehills. Some days I couldn't stop crying, feeling so low; it was unbearable at times. We had to get a birthday present for Paul; his sixth birthday was just a few weeks after Niki died. Dave and I had a disagreement about what to give him. I wanted to get him a bike, but Dave said no, he should learn first on the small one that had been Niki's. He may have been right, but the disagreement was hard to take when feeling so heavy. I needed us to be close, or I couldn't cope. Lord, help us!

We eventually decided on a present for Paul, and I mistakenly decided to go to a shopping centre I was not so familiar with. I got lost in diversions, which was stressful, and then I couldn't find my way out of the car park down into the shopping centre. I thought I was going crazy ... that's how I felt, so often.

WEDNESDAY JULY 1st

Paul was happy on his birthday, with friends home for tea, his grandparents here again, and friends popping in with presents. Something else to be thankful for, in the greyness of the days. There was also a party for Paul, a few days later at the weekend. It was something I felt I couldn't organise, but the people from our church were wonderful, and they suggested having a party for him in the hall there. They organised all the food, and between us we booked an entertainer who did some puppet shows and magic tricks, which went down well with the children. Paul was able to invite most of his class as the premises were big enough and plenty of food was provided, and he loved it. To bless Steve as well, the church gave him a present – how thoughtful.

In those first weeks, I found I couldn't bear to be alone at home. Dave went back to work, and Steve and Paul were at school, so during the day it was just me. I had lovely friends who rang, visited, had me round, but in between I was always trying to fill my time.

Looking back at my diary makes me feel quite exhausted, as I read of all the things I did in one day, between just 9:00 a.m. and 3:15 p.m. For example: I got a new tyre fitted on the car; went to the bank; went home; rang some friends; paid a bill; went to buy a rubber seal for the washing machine; went to the supermarket; went to a friend's for lunch, then to another friend after lunch; and then to school!

By the evening, I would be really tired, and with that came the gloominess, the tearfulness, but at least I had got through another day. It had to be a day at a time, the only way to cope.

As I talked to Dave, we realised that he had got used to being on his own again, with going to work every day, but I was still very dependent on others for company.

Having said that, it was also hard when Steve and Paul came home from school, as the atmosphere was so different without Niki. She was the extrovert – the noisy one. She was the link between her brothers. Without her, they were lost. They weren't used to just relating to each other, as I've said before. Sometimes I longed for an argument, believe it or not, because that was normal – quietness was not! It was so very quiet at times, and it was like we were all lost in this vacuum. I wanted to be strong for them, and help them through their grief, but I was so overwhelmed by my own grief.

Sometimes I would slip out to the garden, and have a cry there. Steve would usually miss me, and come and find me, trying to comfort me. This was the wrong way round, but I couldn't help it. I couldn't be thankful enough for all the friends who popped in or rang, to families who invited us round, or took us out with them for the day. Our family was broken, and we needed constant loving care to get us through. We needed those refreshing springs in the dark valley.

As I read my Bible, helpful words would jump out at me, like "The eternal God is your refuge, and underneath are the everlasting arms."[7] Yes, I was in a dark valley, but I was getting through each day. I did still have my husband and sons; I hadn't completely fallen apart. There were family and friends around me to help, even though they were grieving too, and so often there was a phone call from a friend at just the right moment, when I thought I couldn't cope any more.

When I broke down in tears, there was some relief for a while afterwards. When I shouted at God and told him it wasn't fair it was like he put his arms round me and held me until I felt calmer again.

Other mums at the school would ask me – how do you cope? They were amazed, I think. Amazed that I was managing to do the day-to-day things, like getting the children to school every day. They didn't see me in my darkest times, but on the whole, I was going on with life, I was coping. They knew I had some faith in God. I wrote this poem to answer their question:

How do I Cope?

How do I explain when they ask
What it is that inspires me so,
That makes me so brave to go on
In the face of tragedy, and death?

They say they could never cope
If it were their child that had died;
"You're so courageous, it's amazing –
What is it that makes you so?"

They somehow connect it with religion –
"I go to church sometimes" they say;
But they know it's not enough
When it comes to a crisis like this.

"You've got your faith," they say,
"That's how you're able to cope".
My faith itself is very weak,
But it's faith in a very strong God!

Even that's not enough for me;
It's too impersonal to really help;
(Why, if God is so powerful and great
Did He let my daughter die?)

No, that's not the way I see God —
Someone out there who's remote —
No, my God holds me with strength
But with such tenderness and care.

It's like two enormous hands
Taking a delicate butterfly
And holding it — oh, so tenderly,
So as not to damage its wings.

That's what God's doing with me:
He's picked me up, broken with grief,
He's breathing into me His love
And His peace, to strengthen me.

You see, I know God as my Father,
One that really wants the best for me,
And as I've given my life over to him
I can trust Him to do the right thing.

Yet I don't want to make it sound easy,
I've shouted in protest at God;
I've told Him this isn't fair.
Why has He allowed it to be?

But however much I shout, and kick,
And beat at God's chest as it were,
He just puts His arms around me
And holds me there with love – so secure.

He comforts, He shares the pain,
Yet waits to bring me, through the tears
To a new place, firm ground once again,
With a freshness not known before.

Through the valley of the shadow of death,
With its sad, grey rocky terrain,
To green hills, and rivers and lakes,
Beautiful trees, and flowers, and fruit.

Yes, so much I cannot imagine;
But the most exciting of all
Is that this place is nearer to God
Than ever I was before.

I feel I'm a privileged person;
That through the suffering and tears,
I'll come that much closer to God
And feel, just a little, how He feels.

And this is what God wants for you.
This peace is not just for me;
God wants to hold _you_ in his arms
If you'll give yourself over to him.

He's your maker, He knows you best,
You can trust your life to Him.
And when the worst happens to you
He'll pick _you_ up, and carry _you_ through.

I hoped that writing these poems would help others understand what it was like, and how God could help them through such tragedies too, but it was also a part of my own healing. As I wrote down my feelings, it was letting out some of my grief, and then God would reply to me. As I carried on writing the words down, it was him speaking to me – quite an amazing experience, and it certainly brought some comfort.

He really did care about me, and he never left me, not for a moment, as I walked through this dark valley that I never wanted to enter. Looking back, I am amazed at how I lived through this time, and it was my Father God carrying me that made the difference.

My parents continued to support us, and my Dad was always looking for ways to bring help and comfort. One day, he arrived with a microwave oven. This was a new thing at the time, and something I had not yet acquired. He had American friends who were going back to the US and getting rid of a lot of their belongings. So he got hold of the microwave, and a small TV. The microwave provided a pleasant distraction for me, making cooking a bit different. The TV went to Steve for his bedroom, not such a good distraction in hindsight as it meant he spent more time there, and less with us. Consequently, he may have held in more of his feelings in those early days and had to let them out gradually as he got older.

10

More Hurdles & God's Amazing Ways

THURSDAY JULY 9th

Dave had to go away for work. It was only one night, no problem normally, but now it was like a mountain. I hated being apart from him. I felt so alone, and I was worried about his safety and about Steve and Paul being well while I was on my own with them. You see, I had lived in a bubble where bad things like this only happen to other people. You see it on the news, in the papers, and you feel sorry for them, but it's remote. Now it had happened to us, the worst thing possible had happened to our daughter. Now it could happen again, to any of us.

I came home from dropping Paul at school – to an empty house. This was what happened every day, but this day was different. Dave wasn't coming home this evening. He wasn't so easily available – there were no mobile phones in those days. I saw some of his shoes, left in the bedroom, and suddenly panicked. It felt like he had gone too, like Niki. It was a horrible feeling. I went straight out, got in the car and drove to see Ros, my faithful friend. I had another friend arriving a few hours later, and another one coming to spend the night with me. I'd got it all sorted ... then in the evening Paul started feeling unwell.

He was hot, then he was cold, he had funny pains in his arms. Oh Lord, please look after him. I kept checking on him as he slept. Why did it have to be now? The first time Dave was away. I thought of trying to ring Dave, but what could he do? I'd read in a devotional book that morning – "Always talk to God first about your problems." So I did, and then remembered to give Paul some medicine to lower his temperature. Paul's fever went down within an hour, and I had peace to go to sleep, a greater miracle! I kept him off school the next day though, just in case. He was sleepy and quiet, and I was very protective.

This over-protectiveness affected Dave and me, and took a long time to wear off. Every time Dave was later home than expected, I felt panic. Every time the boys had a minor accident or illness, I felt that dread in my stomach. They all suffered from asthma to some degree, and a few months after Niki had gone, Steve had an asthma attack. He'd never been as bad as Paul, so this was a shock. Nothing seemed to help. Inhalers had no effect and we needed to go to A&E, at the same hospital where Niki had died. Oh Lord, I'm praying again, please look after Steve. He kept saying sorry, bless him; he knew how hard it was for me to go. We had to wait in A&E, as you do, and I got nearly hysterical. I told them my daughter had died there, not long ago, they had to see my son – NOW! I think we got seen sooner than we would have done, just to calm me down.

Thankfully, Steve didn't need to be admitted. He started recovering, still saying sorry to me, as if it was his fault.

Things in the diary were often hurdles. We had to stop and think – can we still go through with this or not? Just a month after Niki died, the diary told us we had a weekend away planned. We had tickets for my university reunion at Warwick University. It was twenty years since I had gone there to study for my degree in Molecular Sciences. It seemed like another world now. It was only a month since Niki had died, and would be really hard, but the positive side was that we would be staying with good friends for the weekend, and we needed the company.

FRIDAY JULY 10th

We set off in the evening, ready for the reunion on the Saturday. I didn't see many people I knew, but some of my old lecturers and tutors were there. I told one about Niki – because I wanted to. Then one I didn't know so well asked how many children I had … oh Lord! I couldn't pretend, cover up, just say two boys, as I would still have burst into tears, so he got the story, abbreviated. He was embarrassed for asking, and I had to pretend it was okay. It was not okay, it was anything but okay. This was to happen repeatedly when I met new people. Why do they ask that? Why do they have to ask that?

After staying with our friends for the night, I wasn't well on the Sunday morning, so I stayed home while the others went to church. I was reading a book written by someone who had experienced a close bereavement[8] and she was writing about the sort of feelings I was having. It helped to know someone else had been through it and understood. It was the same experience of grief coming in waves, and in between feeling detached, forgetting the pain for a while. Then I picked up a Bible, which happened to be Steve's, a different translation to mine. I opened it and read this: "He will carry the lambs in his arms, and gently lead their mothers."[9]

This was referring to the Lord Jesus. Immediately, I remembered my vision, the night when we knew things were really going bad with Niki. I'd seen Jesus carrying Niki up a hill. Now God was speaking to me, comforting me as he promised to gently lead me through this grief. I thanked him from my heart, picturing him carrying Niki and holding my hand. I was close to Niki through Jesus. The amazing thing was that in my own Bible that verse didn't come over in quite the same way, and would not have touched me with such comfort. What an amazing God! He knew just what I needed, and when.

Another big need I had was to visualise Niki in heaven. I believed that was where she was, but how could she be somewhere so far away without me, and somewhere I had never been? I'd always believed in heaven, being taught about it from a small child, but now it was hard to believe it was real.

How could my little girl be in that airy-fairy place, with angels and constant church services? Was it a real place? What was the purpose of heaven? What was Niki doing there?

How could she fit in there? Was she alright there on her own? Who was looking after her?

I thought of my grandparents, but she never knew them. Would she know them there?

Unbeknown to us, a friend had got in touch with a man called Denis Ball. He was an international Christian speaker, with lots of experience with people as they were dying. He would ask them what they were seeing, and seemed to have some special insight into the spiritual realm. As I write that, I want to emphasise that he was not trying to reach the spiritual realm, not at all, but simply asking God for insight into what heaven was like. He gleaned what he could from people who had some vision of it as they passed from this life to the next. (He is now in heaven himself.)

Well, he rang me, out of the blue, one day as I was struggling with these thoughts and doubts. He said he believed I wanted to hear about heaven, and that he had things to share with us. Wow! It was like he was reading my mind. He was writing a book about heaven and felt there was a lot there for us. This was an answer to the cry of my heart: what is it like for Niki in heaven? He said he would pray with us, and that he'd known other families where a child had died and hearing about their experiences might help us.

He invited us to go down to Dorset to meet with him, but he had a very full diary. The only free weekend he had in the whole year – wait for it – was the weekend that we were due to be in Dorset with some friends. How amazing is that!

Meanwhile, as I waited for that meeting, my day to day journey through grief continued. I would keep waking up feeling tired. Was it because subconsciously I didn't want to wake up, because waking up meant facing reality again? While I was asleep I was out of it, but on waking, the pain of our loss hit me afresh every day.

When I managed to read my Bible, there was often something that touched my heart and brought some comfort. One day I read: "in the day of trouble he will keep me safe in his dwelling; he will hide me in the shelter of his tabernacle and set me high upon a rock."[10] That sounded safe and comforting, close to God.

Then: "I am still confident of this: I will see the goodness of the Lord in the land of the living. Wait for the Lord; be strong and take heart and wait for the Lord."[11] We were hanging on to God's promise to bring good out of this. Right from the start of this nightmare journey, Dave and I had been saying to God, this is so terrible that we are looking to you to keep your promise – "that in all things God works for the good of those who love him."[12] We loved him, so he had to bring some good out of this if we were going to make it through.

I would feel comforted for a while, even a day, but life was a series of ups and downs, with more downs than ups. Not long after reading those verses, I was struggling again to keep my head above water. Suddenly death seemed ugly and harsh, as my memory brought back the image of Niki lying on that hospital bed – dead. I couldn't see anything positive then. Oh God, help me, I feel as if I am in deep mud – I can't get out. It's so hard waiting for it to get better. Will it ever get better? How can it, if Niki is never coming back?

The next day I read: "He lifted me out of the slimy pit, out of the mud and mire." That was exactly what I was feeling! That was just what I needed. "He set my feet on a rock, and gave me a firm place to stand. He put a new song in my mouth."[13] I didn't feel it though.

I felt so miserable. I asked Paul's teacher if I could go in and help the class, and she said, "Of course, stay as long as you like." It helped to be distracted for a while, but when I went home again for lunch, I felt really depressed. I played one of Niki's favourite songs, and cried and cried and cried. I asked God for a picture of Niki, and he showed me, in my imagination, Niki leading a whole troop of children and toddlers in a dance around me, with such love in their eyes, and the little ones all putting their arms out to me. I felt such love pouring over me!

The next moment, the phone rang – a friend checking I was in before coming to see me. It was just what I needed. God looking after me again. I cried over her, and she was lovely. I describe that picture, and my friend's timely visit, as a refreshing pool in the desert.[6]

That is how it is. Grief is a dry barren place, grey and bleak, and you have to walk through it. There's no alternative path; but there are some oases there, some pools of water, some springs of clear, fresh water, to drink, to pour over your face. When you call out to God in desperation, he *is* there.

11

Triggers in Grief

As I went through each day, I might be doing quite well, getting things done, like housework. But then something would trigger a memory, and the tears would start again. It might be a photo of the five of us as we were, Niki cuddled up to her Dad. Or seeing her boots. Niki and I had bought identical boots, royal blue, and loved wearing them together. They were still there in the hall, next to mine. I couldn't bear to put them away, like if I did it was too final. If I left them there next to mine, perhaps it wasn't real, she would walk in again.

Ros came up with the twins, and I got Hannah and Rebecca mixed up. It's easily done with identical twins, but I got really upset. I was so muddled after that, I couldn't shake it off. She helped me in the house, bless her. She helped by cleaning Niki's bedroom – now it was Paul's, but it still had lots of her things in there – while I cleaned mine.

Dave came home. I was so low, I let it out with him. I set him off, and we cried together. He said his bad times were walking to and from the station every day, it gave him time to think … especially coming home, and no little girl to run and meet him. It hit him afresh every time he came home.

I felt my heart breaking for him. I'd been so taken up with my own grief. My heart was breaking for Steve and Paul too. I wanted it to be better for them, but we couldn't make it better for each other; we all had to walk through this dark valley. We needed to help each other … we tried. Steve was quiet, not expressing much grief yet. But he would wake up sometimes at night in a panic and stand outside our bedroom – not really wanting to knock and disturb us, but having to. We would do our best to comfort him, not knowing quite what was going on in his head. Paul had tantrums over little things, and these got worse after Niki died; it was all part of the grieving.

One night I had a nightmare – Stevie, as a baby, had been kidnapped. I remember shouting "No! I can't lose another child!" Dave woke me up, trying to comfort me, and prayed with me. He was so understanding, what a comfort.

I read later in the Bible that "his understanding no one can fathom."[14] That was referring to God, but it's such a blessing to have a husband who understands, a small reflection of God's love to me.

I think I was trying to understand all God's ways too soon, trying to work out the good things he was going to bring out of this. It is a journey, and we don't get straight to the destination. It's like children on a journey, always asking "Are we there yet?" Lord, this waiting is so hard.

WEDNESDAY JULY 22nd

My dad went with me to see the headmaster, Mr Hider, about money that had been collected for Niki from staff, children, and parents. They had given the most beautiful white flowers for Niki's farewell, in the shape of a teddy bear, sitting up. But there was so much left over. They wanted to talk to us about what to do with it. It could have been given to a charity, but as we talked, we all felt it would be good to have a visible memorial of Niki. Mr Hider suggested a bench, with a small plaque, to be placed in the quiet playground. That touched my heart. What a thoughtful man he was, helping us through this time. We agreed on the inscription:

> This seat is a gift from
> The children, staff and parents
> Of Derwentwater Middle School
> To the memory of
> NICOLA JOY GATTING
> Who died while a pupil here
> 1977–1987
> The Lord is my shepherd Psalm 23

I then went in to Niki's class, as her teacher had given an open invitation. She had Niki's things ready to collect, pictures she had drawn, etc. It was hard, but the children were all friendly and chatty, and I showed them the photos from our holiday. The last ones of Niki were all so good and special – God knew we would need those beautiful pictures. Several of Niki's friends wanted copies, her class teacher did as well. The letter she had sent us was such a blessing, with memories of Niki that we hadn't seen. She told us what Niki was like at school – quite the leader in organising other children, and even adults at a Maths evening!

When I got home, I thought I would make a lovely rhubarb pie for supper, a treat for Dave. But after the emotional turmoil of the day, I forgot how much fat to put in with the flour, and put in double the amount. It turned out all soft and soggy! It got eaten though, my wonderful husband didn't complain. I wondered again if I was going mad.

THURSDAY JULY 23rd

My friend Sue, who was living just down the road, rang to say her dad had been taken to hospital suddenly the night before. He was in a lot of pain, they didn't know what was causing it. She was off sick from work with a bad cold, and didn't know whether to go down to Sussex to see him. Would it be bad for him with her cold? Later in the day I heard from a mutual friend that Sue's dad had just died. Oh Lord, she didn't get there to see him. More grief.

Sue would often babysit for us, so she knew our family well. These were her thoughts at the time, of Niki and what happened:

> My first memory of Niki is when she was two years old. She sat in her high-chair, dark curls framing her animated face, and carefully said "please" and "thank you" at all the appropriate times.

> As she grew up she became more boisterous and precocious. She had to so as to hold her own with an older, and later also a younger, brother.

> I last saw Niki when she was nine years old. The family, who lived near me, left for Europe on their summer holiday. A few days before they arrived home I flew to Iceland for my two-week holiday.

> Niki's father had said that he would collect me from the station on my return home, so I telephoned from the

airport to tell him that I was on my way. His father-in-law answered the phone, saying that he was staying for a few days and that there were other friends waiting for me at the airport. I asked if anything was wrong and he replied that they would explain when they saw me. I assumed that one of the family was ill, and hoped that it was nothing too serious.

I was glad to see my friends as I emerged from customs. I usually have to battle my way with luggage on public transport, and it was a luxury to be ferried all the way home by car.

"Is anything wrong?" I asked, after being complimented on my healthy appearance (Iceland had been enjoying a heat wave, whilst England had been cold and wet).

"We'll talk in the car," they answered, which increased my anxiety, but nothing could have prepared me for what was to come.

"I'm afraid it's bad news. Niki has died." I was told.

I was still in Iceland in spirit, full of the marvellous time which I had had there. The news was all the harder to take in.

The journey home was filled with a strange ping-pong conversation. I asked for details of Niki's death; then told my friends about my holiday; then, guiltily, asked again about Niki and her family. When we arrived home, I apologised for my insensitivity in talking about my holiday at such a time, but they seemed to understand.

I could not sleep much that night, and every time I woke up I thought about Niki. How could that little girl, so full of life, be dead?

When her grandfather came round the next day, I desperately tried not to cry. He was not crying, so I had no right to do so. Besides, I had a lot to do before returning to work and could not allow myself the time-consuming luxury of grief. It was not so much for the personal loss of Niki that I wanted to cry, but for her parents. They had been my friends for a long time and I felt deeply for them.

Later that day I went to their house. I had no idea what to say, but that did not matter. As I hugged Niki's mother, she amazed me by saying, "I feel so sorry for you arriving back from holiday to this news." I hardly felt that my tragedy equalled hers, but was touched that in her own need, she could think of others.

The funeral was both sad and joyful – a celebration of a little girl's life, but a natural grief which had everyone in tears.

In the cemetery, it poured with rain. Everyone else there seemed to have a partner to cling to. I felt terribly alone as I stood somewhat apart from others, yet I rebuked myself for being concerned with my own feelings at such a time.

Niki's death was a tremendous shock, and having been away during her brief illness I had no preparation at all.

Six weeks later, my father died. He was 64 and had only been ill for two days. I was numbed, as if in a dream, and did not even cry at the funeral. I was supposed to support my mother and could not allow myself grief. Back at work afterwards, I had to be normal. In other circumstances, I would probably have sought out my friends, Niki's parents. But, unreasonably perhaps, I felt that their loss was greater than mine and that I could not add to their burden with my sorrow.

But then death never happens at convenient times.

I think those words reflect how others around us were dealing with Niki's death too.

FRIDAY JULY 24th

This was Steve's last day at Derwentwater Middle School. He had to leave what was familiar to him, and start secondary school in September. I felt for him with all that had happened - his whole world had changed, his family broken apart.

SATURDAY JULY 25th

While the boys were at the sports club, Dave and I started packing up Niki's clothes and putting them in the loft, except her coats and boots. I still needed to hug her coat, and get her smell. I put her bridesmaid's posy in my bedroom. It felt better to have Paul's clothes in his room now, instead of Niki's. He needed that.

Then news came through about a friend's baby being born. The cord had been around his neck, and there was only a 50/50 chance he would survive. No Lord! Please let him be alright. They had already had one baby die. I feel physical pain in my gut.

They called him Joel, meaning "Let God be God".

He died. It was the same thing as the first baby – internal organs pushed up into the lung.

They still say it's not hereditary.

Oh God, it's unbearable. Why?

12

A Summer Break – or Not?

MONDAY JULY 27th

With the school holidays looming ahead, we set off for a few days to stay with Dave's mum in Devon. Usually on this journey, the children loved stopping at a Happy Eater for a meal, as it meant they could play outside, or with the Lego provided inside. It made a good break from sitting in the car. But now the boys didn't want to go outside to play, not without Niki, who was the catalyst and cohesion between them. It was a subdued meal, so different to the times we went there with Niki.

TUESDAY JULY 28th

It was hard going. I had hardly slept the night before, with the noisy road outside, and Dave was like a bear with a sore head as he couldn't stop sneezing all day. We went to the beach and played crazy golf, had fish and chips – all the things we would normally do there, but it was empty.

In the evening, Dave was telling his mum about the funeral, as she had not been able to travel to it, and about the letters we had received, over a hundred. I just wanted to be on my own and retreated to the bedroom to read. Was it selfish? I don't know. Sometimes I had no energy to think of anyone but myself. I spent what energy I had trying to keep the family together and help us have some fun, amidst all the grief.

Dave's mum said her sister had told her she should take down all the photos of Niki before we arrived. She thought it would upset us! Quite the opposite – I would have been very upset if all the photos had disappeared. I guess everyone had their own ideas about what would be helpful to us. Who am I to judge?

WEDNESDAY JULY 29th

We took Dave's mum to Cornwall, to visit close friends, going the long way over the moors. It was three hours in the back of the car for me with the boys. It was hard to have any conversation with Dave's mum as she was stone deaf, and sitting in the front, so could not lip read. Once there, the boys had no confidence to go off and amuse themselves, so it was up to me to go with them while Dave did the socialising. Then I ended up on my own, with just a kitten to cuddle, which was nice. Then the kittens had to go the vet, so I was alone again, in the garden, with no will to make an effort to enter into conversation at all.

Our friends recommended a shorter route back, but Dave still went the long way, causing more tension between us. This whole trip was turning into a disaster.

There was one special moment, though, a ray of sunshine in that day. On the drive back to Dave's mum's, Steve sensed my gloom, as he often did, and started singing to me one of Niki's favourite songs – "Jesus wants to take away your sadness." Needless to say, I found it hard to keep the tears back at that.

I just wanted to go home, and so on Thursday we decided to return, after a trip to the beach. We played bat and ball there, the nearest we got to fun as a family. It still felt like we would never really have fun again. How could we?

We had to go and say goodbye to Dave's aunt and uncle, and when we got there, the engine was hissing – no water in the radiator. The hose had split. Dave would never normally let that happen, but things were not normal any more. His aunt and uncle reprimanded him, saying he should check the water every day. I couldn't take this – couldn't they see that we were in a terrible state? I walked away.

When we got back to mum's house, a man stopped by the car and pointed Dave to the nearest garage. Wow! Was he an angel? It got fixed while we packed, and we got on our way mid-afternoon. We all visibly relaxed as we drove home, and Steve and Paul were happier at the Happy Eater. It was so good to be home. It felt safe and comforting. Within days we had close friends around us again. That was when we felt more relaxed and able to get through each day.

13

A Glimpse of Heaven

MONDAY AUGUST 17th

The day came for our visit to Denis Ball in Dorset, to talk about heaven. Our friends had to cancel the joint trip we had planned, but we were prepared to travel to Dorset for our appointment with Denis – more than ready. It had turned out to be the day before the inquest into Niki's death. That was something we were dreading, as the press would be there, and we had to listen to the details of Niki's death. We just didn't want to go there.

Denis led us into his tiny study, where he gave us the only two chairs and sat on a pile of books himself! That was the sort of man he was. It was a very peaceful place and he spoke to us with such a gentle voice. He told us about being with people as they were dying and he would ask them what they could see. Sometimes they would have a vision of heaven, which he would record. He spoke so confidently about heaven; it was such a real place to him.

He told us about a mother whose daughter had died and she had a vision of her one day, just as she sat at the kitchen table. Her daughter was dancing towards her and her mother called out her name, willing her to come to her. She danced past, as it were, and as she did so her mother realised there was someone with her, another girl, and instantly she knew it was a baby she had miscarried. It was two sisters playing together in heaven! The vision passed, but it had a lasting impact on that lady.

The whole experience with Denis was like a bit of heaven. He prayed and spoke prophetically over us. Here are some extracts:

> The love that comes out of so much pain, hurt, brokenness is a love which is being formed, shaped, it is an eternal love, not a selfish love. It's God's love.

To think of the people we love most is nothing compared with the love we will know there (in heaven) – knowing you are accepted, you are special.

He talked to God just like he was there in the room.

We've been talking about some of the wonderful things you've done and prepared for us; that wonderful experience that is now Niki's, the tremendous happiness and joy she's now experiencing, Lord! She'll probably need a few thousand years to get used to the first dose of it, but you know how to do that, Lord, there's nothing you cannot do; you've got some plans for us ahead, and all to bring us closer to your embrace.

Oh Lord, you have laid your hands upon these two precious people, David and Ruth, and your Spirit is, has been, overshadowing them. Lord, what I would like is that from this day you will very gently by your Spirit touch the eyes of their understanding … I would like, Lord, for the veil to be taken away, for them to see and know and understand as never before, so that, Lord, that sweet, refreshing joy will spring up like a fountain within them, and Lord it will flow out into the heavenly pastures and will meet the wonderful, joyful flow that comes from Niki and all those others that she is part of.

Father, if we could see what they do, if we could see the splendour, the wonderful happiness the delight they take in blessing people … Lord, we're going to see such things one day, that she has seen, and we'll say "Oh Lord! If only we could have seen further!"

Father, please put your hands on these two precious people. Pour into them such assurance … all doubt and fear and sorrow to seep away. Lord, that you will pave that path they tread with beauty and fragrance. Bless them….

As you give of yourselves, so you will receive, this is a basic law of heaven. As you give your heart, as you give your mind, as you give your time, as you give your attention, as you offer it, perhaps often sacrificially, so will God receive it. Beloved, bless and you shall be blessed; give and you will receive. Learn to receive, that you might give and in all things do it as unto him who has done all things well for you.

Where there was but darkness there shall be colour and beauty, and where there was nothingness there shall be shape and form of hills and valleys, streams and all manner of creatures, and it shall be, as you delight in all these things that you see, so will the Lord take pleasure in you, that those things your hearts do desire shall come to pass.

We didn't understand all the beautiful, flowery language, but we left with such a peace in our hearts. As we drove back along the motorway, it seemed more like flying as we were still experiencing a bit of heaven! The inquest the next day seemed of minimal importance, the dread gone. We had been touched by Jesus and our eyes were set on higher things.

The details of the cause of Niki's death seemed immaterial now. She was definitely, amazingly, in heaven! She was like the pioneer in our family, going ahead of us to discover heaven first. She always wanted to be in front, leading us in walks, going ahead … and she was now in her real home, the place that is going to last forever, something we cannot really imagine.

Slowly, gradually, after that, I began to see Niki was in a better life, a much fuller life now than she had ever been in here. She was often bored when she was here, looking for more, for excitement. Now she had it in abundance! I wrote this poem later:

My Butterfly

Caterpillars only crawl, caterpillars only crawl.
But they can move from place to place,
Taste different leaves and plants
Get all the food they need.

They are limited though, I suppose?
I mean, they can't travel miles, can they?
And their lifetime is limited, too;
It has to come to an end.

When the caterpillar's life seems over,
Then a dry old chrysalis is left;
It hangs on a fence or wall
And appears completely dead.

But look at that dead, dry skin;
It's quivering, as if it's alive!
Something is bursting to get out;
What is beginning to emerge?

It has folded wings as it appears,
Entering a bright new world;
It flutters nervously, spreads its wings,
Oh what beautiful colours unfold!

Suddenly it's in the air,
Flying from flower to flower!
No need now to stay near the ground –
It can view the best blooms from on high!

It can fly to laburnum tree,
It can land on a delicate rose;
The caterpillar had no idea
Such a life was waiting out there.

God, is this what it was like for Niki,
As she stepped out of her dead little body?
I'm sure she was a little nervous (where am I?)
So Jesus came to meet her, I know.

I saw the green hills that she loves
And Jesus was carrying her up;
He was holding her close to his heart
As He does with the lambs in his care.

I asked for her to meet with You, Lord,
In a real and very close way,
Before she came back to us here;
I didn't mean for her to stay.

But I guess it was just so good
Being close to Jesus up there,
That she didn't want to come back
Even though she loved us down here.

Does a butterfly look down from the sky,
See her family as caterpillars still,
And say to herself with remorse
"I wish I was back down there"?

Back to crawling around, restricted,
When she's tasted such freedom and life?
No! She waits with excitement and joy
To show us all round her new world!

There's a big gap in **our** little world
Now you've left us for your new life,
But Niki, we're glad you're so happy
In **your** new world – up in heaven!

Once again, it was a poem inspired by God, to help me cope without Niki, to give me hope and comfort, to see things from his point of view.

I had written a prayer to God back in February, thanking him for my family, amongst other things, and acknowledging that:

With the panoramic view he has he leads me in the best way, whilst being right with me and holding me up, comforting and reassuring me in his arms.

With this poem, he seemed to be confirming that to me, as I felt him holding me up, and also, helping me to see that Niki was safe and happy too.

As I kept asking God about heaven, he gave me some glimpses of what it was like.

It's a city of brightest light – not a glaring light that hurts the eyes, and eventually causes a headache. No, it's soft, warm colours of light that make you feel warm, cosy, secure, and yet so free to move around, or to rest!

It's a place where everyone is motivated by love – no envy, no spite and no bitterness. Everyone seeks to serve everyone else; no-one seeks power, there are no underdogs, no injustices. I can walk where I wish, when I wish, with no fear. Everyone I meet loves me with a true, giving love which demands nothing.

The exhilaration of being surrounded by people who love me, who want the best for me, is an ever-present emotion here. The warmth of it is a glow right through my being. I radiate this love, too.

Everywhere is at peace, but no-one is bored. It is not an inactive, sleepy peace but a peace that pulsates through the whole city, which buzzes with life in a completeness, a fullness, where everyone is fulfilled, all the time.

Through everything and everyone, most of all, breathes the presence of the all-lovely, all-loving, shining, glorious, all-mighty God, who emanates every brilliant quality you can think of, and many, many more besides, to infinite proportions!

There is beauty in everything, all around, not just in people. The flowers have such colour, such perfume – from them come such beautiful music, songs giving praise to God! Lions lie down with lambs, animals of such softness, their strength used only to help each other, and us. Birds too, of all colours, join in the songs, the music that gives glory to the King. The music gives rise to dance, bodies move in praise to the King — people, animals, flowers, birds — all with such grace, such holiness, such beauty to give honour to the One who alone is worthy.

Children, babies — all with a special beauty — move with freedom and joy, such joy! Their laughter is music to the King! Their games, their worship — all intermingled as one glorious offering to him.

As new arrivals appear they are welcomed with such tenderness. Words are not needed here — the whole body speaks out love. They are enveloped with love and care, especially some babies and children, I see. Their other life was ended roughly and rudely, with such hate. They receive special love and care here, until their faces glow too, with the love that flows here, the love that rules everything in this perfect, holy kingdom.

Wow! Heaven IS real, and it is an amazing place! I began to get more excited about heaven – why don't we talk about it more?

When we go through dark times, it is hope that keeps us going. When people lose all hope, that's when they go into a depressed state. Can you imagine being in a little boat on the open sea, rowing like mad, with no land in sight? What a nightmare! But what if there is land in sight, and as you row, it slowly appears nearer and nearer, and looks increasingly real and beautiful? Wouldn't it intensify your hope, and give you strength to keep going?

That's what God was doing with me – making heaven more and more real to me. It's an inheritance promised to us. God said, "whoever believes in him shall not perish, but have eternal life."[15] Here on earth, we may receive an inheritance but it is not usually received until someone dies. We don't feel it is right to talk about it or get excited about it beforehand as it would appear that we're wishing the person to die. But with our heavenly inheritance Jesus has already died, to make the inheritance available to us.[16]

Even better, Jesus is alive again to enjoy the inheritance with us! He prayed, "Father, I want these whom you have given me to be with me where I am. Then they can see all the glory you gave me."[17] He is really excited about sharing heaven with us!

Heaven is perfect: no death, no grieving, mourning, crying or pain; nothing impure, shameful or deceitful, no evil, no rubbish, no dirt.

Jesus said before he left this earth that he was going to prepare a place for us. Can you imagine having the perfect home, filled with all the sort of things you find beautiful, situated in the most beautiful place? You could go and live there with the people you most love, and all of you would be perfect, so there would be no family rows or upsets! How would you feel about going home? Apprehensive? Afraid? Or excited?

As heaven becomes more and more real to us, it takes away our fears and gives us hope to keep going through the storms of life, with the expectation of a wonderful place to live at the end. God kept reminding me of the reality of heaven: "No eye has seen, no ear has heard, no mind has conceived what God has prepared for those who love him – but God has revealed it to us by his Spirit."[18]

14

Things Go Public

TUESDAY AUGUST 18th

This was the day of the inquest, something we had been dreading. We had been warned that the press would be there; they look for good stories, unusual deaths – that's their job. But we didn't want to be in the limelight, to be interviewed, and we did not want to go through all the medical details of our precious daughter's death. Further down the path I did, but at this point I was not ready for that.

A friend had prayed for me, that I would be detached from it all on the day. It was amazing, the strength I felt as this day came, just after our visit to Denis Ball in Dorset. I did go through it feeling detached from it all, like on a higher plane. It was two months or more since Niki had died, and that helped. I was thankful for that. Any sooner, and I would not have coped so well, and of course, underneath it all was God's plan and timing. He gave us that day yesterday to hear about heaven – perfect timing. There was also no press intrusion that day.

I was getting a bit concerned about my dad though, at this time. He was often at his doctor's surgery as he did odd jobs for them around the place, and so talked to them about Niki. They seemed to think the blame might lie with the hospital and perhaps we should be looking for compensation. My dad was beginning to get slightly bitter. As for Dave and myself, we could not cope with any thoughts about the doctors being to blame, because that meant that Niki's death might have been preventable. After the event, that is not a helpful thought in the grieving process. I prayed that God would help my dad to accept the situation, and to look for God's hand in it all.

The next day, at 9:15 a.m., the local paper was on the phone, and came round to interview me and take photographs. I felt there was no getting away from it, so best to just get through it. It was hard, as the reporter was very pushy about us looking for answers to why Niki died, as if we should not just accept it, but fight – for what? Nothing would bring Niki back. "Where will you go next?" "How are you going to get your questions answered?" I was glad when they eventually left, but was dreading the report coming out, wondering how much they would twist things that I had said.

Dave rang from work to say that our story was in the national papers – this shook us. I later heard from a friend in New Zealand, who had seen it in the press there. This was weird, but it was an unusual cause of death at the time, the chances of it happening were so small.

I went and sat in the garden, to come to a place of rest again in my thinking. Dave had shown me some Bible verses earlier: "He will keep you strong to the end," and "God chose the weak things of the world to shame the strong."[19] Well, that was for me – that was what I needed. And I did regain my strength again. What an amazing God!

A couple of days later I was up early to go and get the local Gazette. I had been worrying about how the article would come out. It was on the front page, and was not as bad as it could have been, but still did not sound like me speaking.

The huge headline was:

Chance in Million that Killed my Girl
(Acton Gazette FRIDAY AUGUST 21st 1987)

A girl of nine died from gangrene after breaking her wrist in a simple game of tag. Mystery surrounds how Nicola Gatting died five days after a playground fall.

Her stunned parents are still waiting for doctors to answer their questions, but surgeons cannot say how the million-to-one tragedy happened.

An inquest heard this week how germs from a graze on her hand or from an earlier throat infection could have infected her wrist....

Mr Richard Coombes, Consultant Orthopaedic Surgeon at the hospital told the Coroners her injuries were extremely minor; he said a further operation was performed and infection was found. Nicola was put on antibiotics but her condition deteriorated.

Pathologist Dr Phillip Lewis gave the cause of death as brain damage due to toxic shock.

The following week there was another article about Niki in the Gazette, though on page 8 this time:

Death that Rocked a Hospital
(Acton Gazette FRIDAY AUGUST 28th 1987)

Medical experts are at odds over the bug that caused a girl of nine to die from gangrene. Growing alarm has followed confusion over how a normal child at a top hospital could have died from a simple fracture of the wrist.

The spectre of gangrene haunted surgical wards in pre-antibiotic days. It was a name to dread and still evokes an irrational fear.

Antibiotics, continually modified, largely banished the scourge from the Western world. They tackled the deadly infections rampant in hospitals, and won.

Gangrene became a spent force relegated to sufferers from arterial disease. Until last month when a child of nine fell in her school playground. She was playing a game of tag, tripped, and broke her wrist. She was a perfectly normal fit child, good at her school work and popular with her classmates.

Within 24 hours she developed a fever and an overwhelming infection. Two days later Nicola was dead.

Doctors at Hammersmith Hospital broke down and wept with her parents, Ruth and David Gatting. Her death provoked a wave of shock, triggering alarm bells in homes and hospitals.

Doctors believe bacteria from her sore throat infected Nicola's arm causing gangrene. The coroner warned last week we could be dealing with an old bug with a deadly new virulence. He said: "Never in 20 years have I seen a case like this. In the past 12 months, I have seen three."

Apparently, a woman had died soon after childbirth the year before at the same hospital. She had raging septicaemia, caught from her own child's sore throat. And another woman had pricked her thumb on holiday abroad … she too died locally, despite antibiotics.

The press reports went on:

Now doctors are facing a barrage of questions:

Was the bacteria resistant to antibiotics?

Are we facing a new era of superbugs?

Was Nicola's infection connected with dirty hospital wards?

And so the speculation and scare mongering went on. A Sunday paper decided it was a killer superbug called Staphylococcus Aureus. The Gazette laid out the facts:

Fact: Nicola's killer bug was NOT resistant to antibiotics. It was sensitive to the first drug of choice – penicillin.

Fact: The bug was an ordinary Group A Streptococcus – commonly causing throat infections. It was NOT a Multi Resistant Staphylococcus, dubbed superbug, and found in dirty wards.

Fact: Group A Streptococcus is usually destroyed by antibiotics – as it was in Nicola's case. No sign of it was found at her post mortem.

The worrying problem remains. Why did Nicola die from her everyday accident? And why was her infection so severe?

The answer is we don't know….

But at the end of the day, it didn't change anything. Nothing was going to bring her back.

It was difficult though, when people asked us how Niki died, what had been wrong, as it was a complicated answer. We couldn't just say one or two words, and that was it, over. We felt we had to go through the whole story, and that was tiring.

With all the national newspapers touching on our story, it was irritating that some got details wrong, when they all had the same source – like Niki's age, how long she was in hospital, etc. But we tried to let it go, and just get on with working through our grief.

My niece, Jo, came round that evening, with a lovely card of a flower in bud. She had written a verse inside:

> Niki – a flower lent, not given, to bud on earth but bloom in heaven.

I thought it was beautiful, and summed up what we had been seeing of heaven that week, and Niki's new life in contrast with the old one.

Yet it was sad too, because I wanted to see Niki flower, here with me, in our family where she belonged.

15

Surviving

Looking back, I would say that the summer of 1987 was a really sad, grey, empty time. It was so hard. I didn't know how to keep going, and help Steve and Paul through the holidays, when we all missed Niki so much. We were at home for most of the school holidays as we'd had our summer holiday away in May–June with Niki.

So, the school holidays seemed to loom ahead like a long bleak valley to walk through.

I remember taking Steve and Paul to the park one day and playing with them – with a ball, or Frisbee. All I felt like doing was curling up in a ball somewhere and crying my eyes out. I missed my girl so much.

Life was now a bumpy road of ups and downs - many more downs than ups, deep downs, like huge pits in the road that I kept falling into. Yet something seemed to keep me going. I knew I couldn't just give up.

And there were springs in the dark valley, when friends or family came round, or invited us out, and helped us pass another day and take another few steps through the valley of grief.

As I look back now at my journal, it seems that God had been preparing me for this even at the beginning of the year:

WEDNESDAY JANUARY 7th

"My soul finds rest in God alone. He alone is my rock and my salvation; he is my fortress, I shall never be shaken."

"Pour out your hearts to him, for God is our refuge."[20]

THURSDAY JANUARY 8th

I have to start by resting in God, because that involves complete trust on the way, the path I am going to take.

I can't choose that – I take the steps, God directs the path.

FRIDAY JANUARY 9th

"Set your minds on things above, not on earthly things."[21]

Later in the year I read: "If there is no resurrection of the dead, then Christ has not been raised either ... and your faith is useless."[22]

Suddenly these words had meaning just for me. If Niki had not been raised to life, then Christ has not been raised, so my whole faith would be meaningless. Thank you, Lord, for revealing the truth of heaven to me now when I need it so much.

Later on in that chapter of the Bible, the question is asked – "How will the dead be raised? What kind of bodies will they have?"[23] It likens them to plants that grow from seeds.

"They are buried as natural human bodies, but they will be raised as spiritual bodies."[24] The contrast between the body Niki had in this world to the one she has in heaven is like the contrast between a little seed and a beautiful flower, shrub, or even tree. Each seed has a specific plant "body" determined for it, and so in heaven there will be such variety of bodies!

Our present bodies are all we can imagine – how can anything be better? But the splendour of this body compared to our new heavenly body is like comparing a seed or bulb with a beautiful flower. Think of the amaryllis – the splendour of those huge blooms, the height to which they grow, compared with the scruffy bulb it grew from. Oh Niki! How beautiful you must be with your heavenly body!

I am amazed now as I read my journal and am reminded how much God encouraged me and gave me hope to go on as I read the Bible on many of those days. I devoured Bible verses that gave me hope.

I read how God is in the dark rain clouds, he makes them his home.[25] It made me think how when we are in those dark rain clouds, those times of great darkness, like I was experiencing, they sometimes seem to be overwhelming. But that's when God comes close, the closest he's ever been.

So I trudged through the long summer holidays, taking comfort from reading God's promises, yet struggling with day to day living. I wanted to be a good mum for Steve and Paul and to have a good time with them, but it was hard for us all to have fun. It was good for them when they were with their friends; it was a distraction for them for a while. It felt so empty without Niki's liveliness; it was all so flat, just the three of us.

We tried to do things at the weekends when Dave was home, but it was still a real effort for us all. We went swimming, and suddenly I realised it was just me going to the female changing rooms, while the boys all went together to change. I felt so alone. Then Paul slipped by the pool and fell over, and we panicked. Another accident; anything could happen. Life seemed so fragile now, such a thin line between life and death.

It helped when good friends invited us out for days with them, as families. We needed help to pass the days, one day at a time. We couldn't look ahead. It was all too black.

We didn't know who we were any more. What was our family? How could we describe it? We continued to struggle to answer when strangers asked how many children we had. Why did they have to ask that?

We used to talk about our children; we loved to, but it wasn't complete any more. We started talking about "the boys" instead of "the children," but that shut Niki out and we couldn't bear that either.

In September, after the school holidays, I started an evening class to learn German. I had decided this before our trip to the Black Forest, thinking it would be a good challenge for me. I wondered whether I could see it through, but got the strength from somewhere to try.

On my first evening there, as we sat introducing ourselves to those near us, a woman asked me the dreaded question –

"How many children do you have?" I thought quickly that I couldn't cope with explaining it all, so, feeling guilty for leaving Niki out, I answered, "Two boys."

She wouldn't let go. "What ages are they?" Groan.... I told her. She then said, "That's a big age gap!" Anger rose up in me, and I decided, right, she's going to get it now!

I told her why there was a big age gap. It was because my daughter died three months ago. I got satisfaction from her deep embarrassment, I'm ashamed to say now, but I do hope she learned not to be so rude in future. Wrong feelings, I know. Forgive me Lord, but some people!

With October getting near, we saw Niki's birthday looming on 8th October. How were we going to get through it? She was going to be ten, and had been excited about reaching double figures. I felt myself getting lower and lower, feeling that things were never going to be okay again.

We decided that Dave would take time off work, and we would decorate our living room – keep busy, and work through Niki's birthday. It seemed like a great mountain with absolutely no way around it, and no tunnel through. The only way to get past it was to go over it.

Then, as I had a quiet meditative time in the bath a few days before, God showed me a picture of it that helped me see. We didn't have to climb up, trudging and weary, just seeing the next bit of the slope all the time. No! There was a chairlift at the bottom, and we could ride up in it, being restful, at peace. We could feel that lovely, quiet, peaceful atmosphere as it glided gently up. At the same time, we could look all around us, and behind, at the beauty. That beauty is the lovely years we had with Niki as our daughter. They were not all gone and wasted, but they had brought colour and variety to our family life. We were to look at them as given by God, something for which to be thankful and appreciative. We couldn't go back to them, the chairlift goes on, and as it tops the peak we could ride down the other side too. That was all new, but with its own beauty, and as in the chairlift, we would be carried in

God's strength and learn to get something of that aerial view that God has.

Wow! That came out of the blue! I could never have thought up something like that.

WEDNESDAY OCTOBER 7th

My parents were with us, and before they went home we had a time of prayer and remembrance of Niki. I described that picture of the chairlift, which the family appreciated, and I also showed a card I had found written by Niki, saying, "To my family, I love you all very much, love from me." We were all in tears, but it was good to cry together.

THURSDAY OCTOBER 8th

Niki's birthday came, and the post brought a note from Ros, always thoughtful, and a card from another friend. It had a poem in it, which was so beautiful, and so apt that we cried buckets. It is called "Is it well with the child?"

Is it well with the child?

The Letter
Dear Lord,
It is the child – about the child
I'm writing to you, telling all my heart –
My poor torn heart, so tempest-tossed and wild
Left to me desolate.

Faith, sore–eyed and distressed,
Forgets her high behest.
Hope, ready to depart
And only longing remains
As warm and wistful now
As in the days
When little Dancing Feet
Slid down the household ways.
For Lord, you took my child
I do not reason with you, though for that.
But here's my plaint – just this:
I ache for news –

There, in the heavenly bliss,
How is it with the child?
Long days I sat
So still, in the still house, and said no word:
And if you spoke to me, I never heard.

But now, tonight
I sit alone to let my soul indict
This letter to my God
I want to know
About the child – I, Lord, who loved her so.
My spirit always sang
When her dear voice out – rang.
And something in me cried
When small ills came and settled at her side.
I tended her – yes, hair and hands and toes.
I knew her sleeping – waking –
Planned her clothes.
And it is I, Lord – I who ask some sign
Some tidings of the child who once was mine;
For I was nearer her than any other –
Her Mother

The Reply
I have so many things to say
But, yet you cannot bear them, not today –
I know and understand.

The promise that my hand
Shall help and strengthen
Seems far off and strange –
At best a poor exchange
For those remembered days,
For all the dear one's wiles
And pretty ways.

Yet let your spirit come to me – to me.
There is no other in the universe
Who can your comfort be.
For who in all the universe

Could prove so skilled and fit
To mollify the broken heart
As he who fashioned it?

You sat so still, and wondered all the while
How she would fare
Without your kiss – your smile;
You were so joined to her, you half forgot
That I was there.

I comprehended her when you could not,
But was I unaware?
That anguished night
Before this darling came
You cried to me
You called upon my name
That helpless passionate word
I, the Life – giver heard!

And you poor wrestler
Found your faith prevail.
The little ship set sail.
Yes, ventured forth into life's stormy sea,
Bound by the limits of mortality.

Listen, Poor Heart! That far off hour is past,
I am the First. Also, I am the Last.
I gave her first faint breath
And in the hour of death
I wrapped her round
And held her – held her fast.

Down all the ages, not a fledgling bird
Has fallen as it flew
But I, its Maker, felt my being stirred.
I – the All Loving – knew.
The child – the child – is by me.
She walks the glory side of me.
So to the poor broken- hearted Mother
News of the child?
How is it with her?

Where in God's high heaven?
What is she doing there?

Why, if I told you, if I let you see
The radiant joys she has for company
If I should draw aside
The curtain –
Leave the casement open wide
For just one moment –
Flesh and blood would fail.

So in his love
The Father hung the veil.
Some blessed day
It shall be rent in twain,
And you shall come
Into your own again.

Oh wavering heart!
Then let this thought enfold you;
That if it were not so
I would have told you.

Until that day, that hour of joy so sweet,
Can you trust me with little Dancing Feet?

(Author unkown)

After tearfully reading that, Dave and I got ourselves together again, and went on with the decorating. As we worked, our spirits slowly lifted. We felt the chairlift! In the evening, the four of us went out for dinner, somewhere different where we hadn't been with Niki. We ate too much, but we actually had some fun.

THURSDAY OCTOBER 15th

The night of the great storm of 1987. It hit south east England severely, with hurricane force winds gusting up to 100mph. Amazingly, we heard nothing of it in the night, but woke to no electricity and wondered why. When we looked out at our back garden we were shocked to see that our lilac tree was uprooted and lying on the lawn. It may not sound much, but to me it was devastating. That tree was a favourite of the children. It had a rope ladder which they could climb or use as a swing. It had become my special place, my refuge, where I went when I couldn't keep the tears back, to cry alone, and now it was gone. It felt like an added bereavement.

In grief, it is so easy for something simple, like the loss of the tree, to tip the balance between coping and falling apart.

A few days after the storm, I had a black day. I did not want to be with anyone, or even speak to anyone. If the doorbell went or the phone rang I was not going to answer it. Yet I felt lonely, desperately lonely. My best friend, Ros, had other commitments that day. I was wallowing in self-pity, like a hippo in the mud.

I called out to God to help me, the only one who could. But he could have stopped the hurt of Niki's death and he didn't, did he?

"What do you want of me?" I shouted to God. "Everything is shaken, even my garden, my tree!"

As I yelled at God, it was like I wrote in my poem, ("How do I cope?") that:

> However much I shout, and kick,
> And beat at God's chest as it were,
> He just puts his arms around me
> And holds me there with love, so secure.

I turned to my Bible again, as that was a place where I often found comfort. I saw some words in a Psalm that could have been written by me: "Be merciful to me, O Lord, for I am in distress; my eyes grow weak with sorrow, my soul and my body with grief.... Come quickly to my rescue, be my rock of refuge.... Since you are my rock and my fortress, for the sake of your name lead and guide me. Free me from the trap that is set for me, for you are my refuge."[26]

As I made this my prayer, I began to feel peace in my spirit. I still had a bad head, but I was on my way up again from rock bottom.

The Rocky Road of Grieving

As we went on in our journey of grief, one thing to deal with was the memory, the flashbacks, of Niki lying ill and lifeless. It was hard to see back past the week she was in hospital, to see the good memories. We had the photos of her, lots of photos, but in our minds the most vivid images were of her in a coma. Someone prayed with us about that, seeing it as cords wrapped around us that needed to be taken off. This happened gradually over the ensuing weeks. We started being able to recall the happy memories of Niki.

I've written about my friend Ros, and the amazing support she gave me through these months. Then in October she told us that she and her husband felt it was time to move out of London. They could not afford to buy a house here, and were planning to move to the south coast. I knew in my mind it was right for them, they needed to get a bigger place, but my heart was heavy. I felt scared, like someone was taking a life support away from me. It was as if I was on a rope bridge across a canyon, and it went on for ever – I couldn't see the other side. That is what grief is like – there seems no hope of it coming to an end. As Dave and I prayed together, the bridge got shorter in my imagination, and peace came back, with hope. God is faithful, and he never leaves us or moves away.

The imagination can be used for good and bad – to conjure up sad or happy things. My dad, at this time, was finding it hard to picture Niki being happy in heaven. He could not imagine a child there being alright, not knowing anyone, and missing her family. He often pictured her looking around for a friend, and then tried to convince himself that she really is completely happy. Later he had a sort of vision, seeing Niki at the end of his bed, and he knew without a doubt that she was very happy! A special answer to his questions and doubts.

I would say here that the bereaved often see images of the loved one that has died. It may be someone they see in a crowd, whom they mistakenly think is that one. It may be like my dad saw, a figure that seems to be there for a moment and then is gone. More common are the dreams of the one that has died, which seem to be a mixed blessing.

I would have a dream where Niki appeared, quite naturally, in the story, and I would think how wonderful that she hadn't gone away for good after all. I would try to get near her, and hold her, but it was never possible. She would leave again, just disappear. You can imagine the fresh grief on waking.

My birthday came, 8th November. I got through it quite well, with friends round, a special cake for me, and watching a film with a happy ending. Then in bed I felt suddenly, desperately sad. It just washes over, with no warning.

Oh for news of Niki, I miss her so much!

So the rocky road goes on, with its ups and downs.

I read these words in the Bible, God promising "To comfort all who mourn, and provide for those who grieve in Zion – to bestow on them a crown of beauty instead of ashes, the oil of gladness instead of mourning and a garment of praise instead of a spirit of despair."[27]

"Ashes" gave the impression of shame, and sometimes I felt like hiding, not showing my face, as some people don't understand grief.

"A crown of beauty" meant to me that I could hold my head up high, with confidence.

"Oil" spoke to me of loosening up, so I determined not to get stiff and stuck in mourning, but to be loosened up, softer, more pliable, and hopefully altogether more useful.

"A garment of praise" sounded good, instead of despair. Despair is a dark, lonely place, not somewhere you want to stay. Praise takes you out of yourself, whether it's praising another person for something or praising God. It's acknowledging something good in someone else, and that lifts the one doing the praising as well as the one being praised. Praising God and acknowledging his greatness meant sacrificing my own feelings, and in doing so, I was lifted out of my hopelessness because God is above it all.

Having said that, I was under no illusion that my grief would dissipate overnight. But I knew that as I walked the journey of grieving I could hold these promises close to my heart, and in the darkest times they gave me hope instead of despair.

The next hurdle was looming: Christmas Day.

How to get through this one? That was the question.

We planned to do things differently, as we could not begin to imagine how to do the same things but without Niki, an integral part of our family.

Instead of a Christmas lunch, we would have an evening meal. Instead of eating in the dining room, we would carry the table into the living room. We would invite others to the meal, namely two nurses we knew, who were on duty for the day but free for the evening.

Then circumstances took over. Paul and Steve got a tummy bug just before Christmas, and then I went down with it too. Great! Preparing food when feeling sick is not good. Then the washing machine decided to break down, pouring water all over the kitchen floor on Christmas Eve.

In the midst of all the mess, it actually didn't seem like Christmas at all. Perhaps that was a help?

We got through Christmas Day, trying to give Steve and Paul some fun, and were all able to eat a bit again after the sickness. We started to relax over the next few days, and as we did I found myself to be very tired and sleepy, unnaturally so, as I began to let go of the tension and effort of trying to keep everything together for the family over Christmas. Then I got a toothache, an infected tooth. Lord, have mercy!

It came to New Year's Eve, and suddenly Dave and I found ourselves panicking. We thought we'd got through Christmas and that was it – done! Now we were being encouraged to look back over the past year and enter into the New Year.

Looking back was very painful, but at the same time we didn't want to leave 1987 because it felt like leaving Niki behind.

Looking ahead to 1988? We couldn't look further than the next day really, as it all looked so bleak and endless. Our huge loss was becoming real now, and was going on for ever. So, it was with heavy hearts that we entered the New Year.

17

Why Did God Allow This?

I was reading in my Bible where it promises that if we make God our refuge no harm will befall us, he will save us. That was hard to take, because a terrible thing *had* befallen us, and God did not save us from it. But as I read on, it promises that God "will cover you with his feathers, and under his wings you will find refuge; his faithfulness will be your shield."[28]

FRIDAY JANUARY 15th

That's what I lean on, when I feel as I do now, that I'm taking one step forward and two back – it's the faithfulness of my God that keeps me going, that protects me from the devil's onslaughts. Thank you, Lord, for your faithfulness. You will not let me go, I declare it. You have got a special purpose for my life, and you will bring it to fruition. Thank you, Lord.

MONDAY JANUARY 18th

I can't understand these promises of protection against all harm and disaster. No one is exempt from it in this life! I think it has to be seen from God's viewpoint, and his perfect plan. He can take the terror out of it for us[29] so that we don't lose our sanity in the disaster.

The Lord says, "I will rescue those who love me. I will protect those who trust in my name. When they call on me I will answer; I will be with them in trouble. I will rescue and honour them."[30]

That last verse is important to me, and realistic ... God is right there in the midst of it with me, and he will bring me through it with glory. That's the most realistic promise in that Psalm for me – it demonstrates that faithfulness of God. He is my shield all around me in trouble, so that I don't feel the full impact of the disaster. Thank you, Father.

So I called out to God – "WHY THIS PATH, LORD?" and the very next day, I sensed that he seemed to say in reply:

TUESDAY JANUARY 19th

"I need you to walk through the valley, on the way to the highest peaks. It's not because I don't love you enough, that I leave you to walk through the dark valley. It's because I love you so much that I take you through the valley. I haven't left you. Even my only Son, my beloved Son, had to go through the dark valley, and I had to leave him alone – can you imagine the pain that was for us both? You only know a fraction of that pain; I had to go through it – for you. My Son had the choice, even though it meant bearing the agony of being completely alone.

You, my children, are not alone. I have never left you for one moment. I could not give you the choice of the way to take, because you could not have made this choice. But I prepared you both through the years, for this road, and I've brought you here because I love you so much. You are precious to me, you are special, and I will not leave you in the valley. I am implanting a special love in your hearts, in a depth that you could not have if you bypassed this valley.

You will come through the valley with such tenderness, with an unselfish love, a love that joins your heart with others; you will have a strength that you never experienced before, and such a closeness with me, it excites me! Your hearts joined with my heart, so that we can commune together as never before. I will use you as friends that I can trust. I have shared my pain with you, in a small measure, but I will share my heart with you, in a large measure. I want you to overflow with my joy, bubble over with my love; I want my peace to leak out of you to those I will put near you."

God seemed to impress on me that this was real, that he was working in our lives through all this pain, and it would be used for good, to help others.

"It is my work, and I will do it in my way — but be ready. Keep looking up, not at things around you. I am above all that — I can change it in an instant; but you must be ready. Walk where I tell you to walk; do what I tell you to do. Be as one heart together — I made you to be one. Remind each other of my work, and be ready!"

I felt so much lighter in my spirit after that! God said it's real, and he's doing it now, and I believed it. How else would my spirit have been lifted? Certainly not by making it all up!

I continued to have conversations with myself, and with God, as I tried to see what my readings from the Bible were saying. What did they mean for me?

WEDNESDAY JANUARY 27th

"Your attitude should be the same as that of Christ Jesus."[31]

He came to earth as a mere man, was tried unjustly for crimes he did not commit, and sentenced to death by a cowardly judge. Through all this he was silent and calm, knowing his Father was in control, even though it meant suffering and pain for him. He knew he was in his Father's will. Because of his obedience and complete submission God exalted him...

So what about my attitude? I may feel I've been unfairly sentenced to life without my daughter, but I need to keep in mind that Father God is in control, and although it means a lot of suffering, he has the overall plan and is working out the best from his viewpoint.

MONDAY FEBRUARY 1st

"I am being poured out like a drink offering on the sacrifice."[32]

That's how I feel.

Giving Niki up to You, Lord, is an enormous sacrifice for us — almost too great to bear — yet in it I feel You want us to be open, transparent even, that others may be able to feel a little of the pain and agony, that others may learn how to care for us, how to understand, and others who also suffer may know that we know what it's like.

Yes Lord, it's like being poured out as a drink offering — on top of the sacrifice. Help us, Lord — with strength directly from your throne — to bear the load with you.

We've longed for someone who's experienced this pain to be there to help us through, to counsel and give guidance. But instead you've only allowed us those around us — so that they may learn to care. Thank you for them.

18

The 'Firsts' Without Niki

As we went on along the path of grief, it was full of pot holes. Pot holes which we would fall into, then come back up again, then walk for a while, before falling into another one. As time goes on in grief, the space between these pot holes gets longer, with occasionally little 'highs' in between.

As I've said before, it was a comfort to know that Niki was remembered, and something happened in February 1988 to cheer our hearts. We received a letter from the Area Recreation Office, as it was then. Niki had been a member of a gym club in a local school, which she loved going to on a Saturday morning with Steve, and Paul too when he was old enough. It was good for them, both as exercise and to mix with other children with similar interests, and also for us, as they used up a lot of energy! Having said that, it was sometimes followed by other activities as a family, like swimming, walking, or going to the library.

The letter was a lovely surprise. It was from the manager, whom we saw regularly at the club. He said that their annual gymnastics awards were coming up, and he would like to have a trophy that is presented annually to the most improved gymnast of the year. He wrote: "I would very much like to name it after Nicola, and it could be known as the 'Nicola Gatting Memorial Trophy.' Nicola was very special at the club, and this would be a mark of how we felt about her and how she contributed to the life of the centre." Wow! That was special.

He invited us to the ceremony and said he would be honoured if we would present the trophy. We did go, and I got Dave to present the trophy, as by then the sadness of the occasion had come over me, as well as the honour in memory of Niki. Then it was Dave's turn to have his photo in the local paper.

In the first twelve months after Niki's death, there were a lot of hurdles – the first this, the first that, without Niki. It started with Paul's birthday, then Niki's birthday, family birthdays, then Christmas, New Year, Mothers' Day, Easter.

Mothers' Day. I was very low the day before, anticipating the difficult day. I coped with it, though, and we had lunch out as a family, but missed Niki so much. My family was incomplete now. I so missed my little girl, who would usually make me a special card for this day. At the same time, I did so appreciate and love my sons, Steve and Paul. I know especially now how blessed I am to have them. They would often show their love and care for me, especially when Dave was away for his work, as together we tried to help each other to adapt to being family without Niki.

Each time one of these hurdles, or pot holes, loomed near, our emotions would start to plummet. It was the anticipation of the difficult days to get through that was often the worst. When the actual day came, we got through it, and were able to start coming up again.

As June 1988 approached, we started reliving the events of the previous year. This time last year we were on holiday with Niki, that wonderful holiday in the Black Forest. This time last year we were on our way home. This time last year Niki fell and broke her arm. We didn't want to go there again, but we couldn't help it. That's the way our minds went.

June 10th came, and Dave had the day off work. We had some phone calls, cards, and notes as those close to us felt for us on this day. The two of us went out to Marlow while the boys were at school. We were actually quite excited, as if we were sneaking off for our first date! It was surprisingly good, after all the fearful anticipation. It must have been help from God, and the comfort of knowing people were thinking of, and praying for us. We then picked up Steve and Paul from school and drove down to Southampton, to stay with our friends Chris and Ros for the weekend. We needed the company. We couldn't face this time alone as a family.

We had a lovely time there, even some time on the beach as it was so warm. But I had toothache on and off – why does it always come when it's already a difficult time? We got home on Sunday evening, and the toothache kept me awake all night. I saw my dentist the next day, and he refilled a tooth, but it made no difference to the pain. I was in agony for another night. Then it was back to the dentist for root treatment, and with painkillers I was able to have a good night's sleep and wake up with no pain. So my mind was taken off the pain of the anniversary I didn't want – of losing Niki – by physical pain.

As the year went on, we started making plans for a summer holiday. This would be our first real holiday without Niki, another big hurdle. Will they never end?

We have long standing friends who emigrated to Canada – Dave had known Ron since primary school and they stayed friends. Ron and his wife Judith were very upset about Niki, and felt a bit helpless being so far away, but they invited us to go and visit them as a family. They felt that was something they could do to help us, and all we had to do was get our flights out there and back. They had a large house, and plenty of room for us all. We started planning it for August, and it was good to have something to look forward to that year. Steve and Paul were really excited. This would be their first experience of flying, and a seven-hour flight. Paul thought he might see Niki on a cloud on the way!

Niki never got to know what it was like to fly – not in an aeroplane anyway. That made me sad, but then, she flew to heaven! Wow!

The boys loved the experience, and Paul especially liked the meals on the plane, with all the little compartments. I just realised afresh, with the magnificent views from the plane, how *BIG* God is.

We arrived to a 30 degrees centigrade heat, so it took us a while to acclimatise and get over jet lag. A few days later we had an afternoon on a beach by a lake, but as it was cooler and cloudy we were caught out – not enough sun cream. I was mortified the next day, when I found Paul on the bathroom floor, feeling rather weak. His back was sunburnt and he was suffering from sunstroke. What a terrible mother I was – why didn't I think? You'd think I would be more careful, after losing my daughter. I missed Niki so much, and she would have been mothering Paul while he was feeling ill, and keeping him distracted and amused. It fell to me to do that alone, while Dave kept Steve occupied and having fun.

It was an up and down time for me – some lovely highs, like visiting Niagara Falls, and at other times, the lows, missing Niki so much. Our friends were wonderful, taking us round, and even to stay for a week in a cabin in a huge wild park up north. But they couldn't take the pain away, and when friends came round with their three daughters, two of whom were twins about Niki's age, it was too much for me. I'd lost my only little girl, and they had three. Fortunately, their garden was so big I could lose myself in it, and have a good cry when I couldn't hold it back. It was so hard being on holiday without Niki, so very hard.

And guess what – I broke a tooth, and had to go to the dentist! Can you believe it? Grieving, as with all emotion, does affect us physically I'm sure, and with me it was my teeth that suffered.

This time it was while we were in the cabin, with only a small town nearby, but thankfully it had a good dentist. Later that day we saw a porcupine crossing the road and chipmunks in the car park. We finished the day toasting marshmallows over a fire on the beach by the lake, so there was fun in amongst the pain and sadness. Oh, and I also fell down the last two stairs – back at Ron and Judith's home – and sprained my ankle!

We loved Niagara Falls so much that we hired a car and went back there as a family for two nights. We enjoyed watching dolphins, sea lions and even killer whales at a large water park, then Dave took Paul on the world's largest roller coaster – and wished he hadn't! He was a whiter shade of pale afterwards, and he has a strong stomach. Paul thought it was 'brill'! Niki's adventurous spirit definitely lives on in him.

Two days later we were flying back to the UK, about midnight, arriving home around midday on September 2nd. We'd been away for four weeks, and on the whole, it was a good time and left us with some lovely memories. It was certainly better than being at home all that time during the school holidays, wondering what to do.

So that was another hurdle over.

19

Emotions along the Grieving Journey

Talking about my loss was necessary, and part of the healing process, and fortunately I had some good, listening friends and family. My sister-in-law had not lost a child, but she had gone through a divorce from my brother, which is very much like a bereavement. I found it so helpful spending time with her, having walks in the country, just talking about how I was feeling, and trying to cope without Niki. She understood and she cared, and also helped me in practical ways.

Talking to someone else who had suffered the loss of a child was helpful too. Sharing with my friend who had lost two babies soon after birth was bittersweet, desperately sad, but we had such understanding for each other. We could share our feelings openly together, which to others would be too much.

Often people don't know what to say to you after such a loss, but they have this need to try and make you feel better, so they say something – sometimes awful things, without realising it. I don't blame them – I was there once, on the other side, the outside of the grief. But now I was in the centre of it, a place I never wanted to be.

I would have things said to me like "She's in a better place." How could that be? What place is better for her than in our family? Later on, I was able to appreciate the reality of heaven, but not in the first stages when this was said to me.

Someone from an extreme religious group gave me a note which told me that God chastens those whom he loves. Ouch! Was that supposed to give me comfort?

"It's good that you have your other two children." Yes, but it doesn't change the fact that I've lost a child. I understand that too now, as I hear of families where more than one child has died, or an only child has died. It *was* a blessing and a comfort to have my two wonderful sons, and it still is – I thank God for them constantly. But in the early stages of grief to have that spoken over you, it can come across as if the child that died had little value.

"You can have another child." That is not necessarily true, and if I did, I would be desperate for another daughter. How would I have felt if it was a boy? And it doesn't fill the gap, like it might help by getting another pet when one dies.

"I know how you feel – my granddad died last year" (he was elderly). Do you? My grandma died when she was one hundred and one. That was very different to my daughter dying. I know it's sad to lose a grandparent, don't misunderstand me. But it's the last generation, not the next, and they have had much of their life. You can't compare bereavements, it doesn't work like that.

"Time heals." This is a favourite comment, and in some ways, it's true, but in other ways it's not. Time passing doesn't automatically heal, but as time passes, it's possible to heal. It depends on the bereaved person's attitude. I've seen people who don't want to let go of their grief, who just stay immersed in it, with no intention of moving on. They want to remain as the victim, and have people's sympathy for ever. There are ways to help ourselves out of the pit, but we must want to move on.

I remember some years later I was counselling a lady whose second husband had died. It was desperately sad; they had only been married a short time, and it looked hopeless. How could she get through this? With some inspiration, I suggested she think of something each day to be thankful for, in her case, to thank God for. She took this on board, and it started her journey out of the darkness. I'm not saying that is a general rule, but it is known that being thankful releases positive endorphins in the body, producing health and encouraging happiness.

Dave and I learnt, when seeing people for the first time who didn't know about Niki's death, that the first thing we needed to say was, "Don't feel you have to say something, just give us a hug!" That's all we needed – to know that they cared. We had to tell them how to treat us – we had to help others help us. For us, physical touch was very comforting, one of our love languages. That will not be the same for everyone, I hasten to add.

Close family and friends were a great help at this time, doing practical things whilst sharing the grief. There were lots of flowers arriving, all sent with love and the best of wishes, but the endless flow can become more of a problem than a comfort, as there are not enough vases and places to put them! I remember a small hand-picked posy from the mother of one of Niki's friends meaning a lot to me – it doesn't have to be expensive bouquets. Friends who invited us out at weekends helped us a lot, as it seemed unbearable to be on our own as a family. We needed people around us.

Grief is the reaction to loss and the process of adjustment to that loss. It is making real inside oneself an event which has already happened and involves a complex mixture of emotions.

There are various stages of grief, and though at the time it was not something I knew or recognised, looking back I can see how we passed through these on our journey – the journey no one wants to take. They vary from person to person, of course, and there is no set pattern, but there are some common emotions.

At first there is shock, and for me it caused panic, as things started going rapidly out of control after Niki's accident. I can't put into words the fear, tension, pain and grief that I felt, as I tried to take in what was happening to my lively, healthy nine-year-old, who was so close and loving to me. I know now that these were all normal emotions brought on by the shock.

Apart from the grief which Dave and I shared deeply and closely, as parents we needed to be there for our two sons in their grieving. How could we help them? We couldn't make it better. I felt as if my heart was broken into pieces and would never be healed. Grieving together as a family was vital, yet seeing the deep grief of my husband was so painful. I'd never seen him cry before. I also felt the grief of my sons, and felt guilty that they had lost their sister and I had not been able to prevent it. That was also a big thing for Dave, as he saw himself as the protector of the family, yet he hadn't been able to stop this awful tragedy.

Yet after the last farewell to Niki, then just a shell of the child I had borne and nurtured, I felt a strange relief. The worrying was over. There was nothing worse that could happen now. I felt a complete nothingness. All my strength had been sapped out of me. I was utterly exhausted. I think the physical weakness caused me to fall asleep each night, but I would wake early in the morning, and the reality of what had happened would hit me afresh. I relived the shock and felt the pain in my chest again, jolting me into complete wakefulness as the tension and grief came flooding back.

There is denial too: this cannot possibly be true; it's not happening; it can't be. There's an inner tension – I don't want this to be true, but it is true. With the physical weakness, emptiness, and inner tension there may well be problems sleeping and loss of appetite.

As those first few days pass there is often a numbness, almost an emotionless state, feeling like a zombie just going through the motions of living. It may act as a defence mechanism preventing the magnitude of the loss from sinking in. I believe this inner numbness – a reaction to the shock – is God's way of giving our system a chance to recuperate, to get through those first days without losing our sanity. How else could we have managed to collect a death certificate, choose a coffin, and arrange a burial place for our precious daughter? In that numbness, I also got through the necessary preparations for Niki's farewell service, being able to make decisions about songs and flowers, and notifying so many people. The numbness we feel in this first stage of grief helps us to do all that we need to do as we try to believe and make real what has really happened.

When we go through dark times we *can* get strength from God to carry us through. We don't get it in advance, in fact we think we could never cope with something like that until we are in it. In some ways we have no choice, but we do, and some make the choice to give up on their lives.

Some may feel abnormally calm and appear to be brave and coping well. I've seen this at funeral services, when those close to the one who has died seem to be fine, and enjoying meeting many friends and family. It's a celebration of the one who has died, and usually such lovely things are said about that person! It's easy to enjoy and to feel proud of their loved one. Then it's all over and it's back to the silent house and the awareness of what has happened starts sinking in.

Then there is yearning, such a deep longing for the lost one, such emptiness. This can be felt as a physical longing, in the chest, or the stomach, physical pain. With this comes surges of deep uncontrollable emotion, weeping, and wailing. I certainly had many times like that, when it was impossible to hold back and crying gave some release to the pressure building up inside, for a time.

I felt enormous yearning for my daughter, my arms aching to hold her again. I found some comfort in hugging her soft jacket at those times, and crying until there were no tears left. The pain increased when I saw girls her age with their mothers, or heard someone call the same name, as it intensified to me what I had lost.

Often there is a replaying in the mind and imagination of the events leading up to the death. There may be feelings of guilt and self-reproach, with a strong desire to change the events or decisions that were made, that would perhaps have brought about a different result. I kept reliving those days in the hospital, feeling guilty for the things I had said, or not said, to Niki. If only I had known she was going to die, I would have treated her with so much more care, I kept thinking. I would never have left her side while she was still conscious.

"What if...?" and "If only..." are frequent questions of the bereaved, also "Why?" and "Why me?" I understand the "Why?" question. I asked God that, shouted at him at times. It's normal, and God can take it! But the "Why me?" question – no, I never asked that, because in asking that I would be saying it's okay for other people to suffer tragedies like this, but not for me – ah, poor me. There is no reason why I should not suffer a tragedy in this life, where people suffer terrible traumas all the time. It's not something I would choose, obviously, but it is not something I can think myself immune from either.

Some said to us, "What if the hospital had given Niki antibiotics as soon as she was admitted?" We saw no point dwelling on that, because it's not something you think of when someone breaks a limb.

There may well be anger, perhaps over possible negligence or harm to the deceased by medical services or the person who may have caused the death. My anger was directed towards God at times, for allowing it to happen when he could have prevented it. But because I have a relationship with him, each time that emotion arose it was eventually overcome because I knew he had such great love for me and trusted that he knew what he was doing. Some are angry with the one who has died, whether that is logical or not. There may even be feelings of anger towards other people who have what the bereaved has lost. Imagine a mother who has lost a baby hearing of another mother who has abused or even killed her own child.

As the months go into years, and it becomes more and more real, the despair and depression can set in, probably the longest stage of grief. The support from people around the bereaved is likely to be waning. They cared, they were there for you, but they expect you to be better by now. They might be appearing to avoid contact with you.

I described it in my journal, as I claimed God's promises:

TUESDAY FEBRUARY 28th 1989

"God comforts us in all our troubles, so that we can comfort those in any trouble with the comfort we ourselves have received from God."[33]

God does comfort us in all our troubles – TRUE!

"This happened that we might not rely on ourselves but on God, who raises from the dead."[34]

God _does_ raise the dead — Niki is alive in heaven!

"He will deliver us. On him we have set our hope that he will continue to deliver us."[35]

God _will_ continue to deliver us — from the intensity of pain, the agony of isolation in the midst of people, of loneliness, unhappiness which no one understands.

God, my Father, if one of these promises is true, if two are true, then they must all be true. So I hang on to them for all I'm worth and cry out — God, deliver us from our hurt and sadness. Fill us with your love, your peace, your joy as you promised. Please give us the help we need, so that we may not wither up and die, but grow and be fruitful.

Reading that now, it sounds like I was pretty despairing at the time. With my closest friend now living much further away, I couldn't see where my main ongoing support was going to come from.

SATURDAY JULY 29th

With Dave away for a few days I wrote:

I must use the time positively or else I will sink into depths of despair (very easily).

It felt like friends were avoiding me, not wanting to get into a long conversation with me, on the phone or in person.

Why don't people say if it's not convenient, instead of giving me the brush-off? I guess our spiritual state puts people off. The sad thing is that we _need_ help, we _need_ fellowship, but when we look for it, well, it's like trying to get hold of a shadow. Shadows aren't very reliable — always changing. We need the real thing, Lord, and I guess that's only found by coming close to you.

Am I full of self-pity, wanting people to treat me like I am wrapped in cotton wool, in case I get more hurt? Do I want to be treated in a special way for ever, or do I want to begin life again, building on the tragedy and trauma I've suffered by using it for good, by helping others through similar situations?

I need to discover how, with my security based in God alone, I can relate to other people and make relationships again, which I am avoiding at the moment.

TUESDAY AUGUST 1st

Ok Lord, so you have a sense of humour! You sent Peter and Helene over last night, unannounced, didn't you? You also told them how low we were, and even that I felt rejected, because they prayed for us in such a gentle loving way, about knowing the peace of God and about being fruitful and a blessing to many. Oh Father, thank you for your refreshing presence, that they brought with them, they were angels sent from you!

There was also a phone call from another lady, a widow, who understood how I felt and we had a lovely chat. God was still on our case, providing the help we needed on the rocky path with its ups and downs.

We seemed to be going through a time of despair that year.

THURSDAY AUGUST 3rd

I wrote about Dave:

I'm not as worried about me as about Dave. He's in the depths of despair, the slightest thing I say upsets him. He takes every comment as criticism, says he's being got at, and feels no one can help him. I know he's hurt, but he keeps taking on more hurt when it's not meant as hurt.

We were both so sensitive in our pain, and there seemed to be a spirit of apathy and despair over us, like a black cloud we could not get out of. It wasn't helped by difficulties in our church situation, with a change of leadership.

I tried to keep praying.

I read: "He redeems my life from the pit and crowns me with love and compassion."[36]

I turned that into a prayer – how we needed that.

Self-pity can creep in and put a bitterness into the grieving person, who feels "Poor me! Don't people realise what I am going through? No one understands." I was feeling that, and very sensitive to people's behaviour towards me when it did not seem to be one hundred per cent caring about me. I had to talk myself into admitting the truth, in my journaling, and not think about myself all the time.

After all, there was always someone going through a bigger tragedy than I was.

As time went on, and disasters hit the news – like the Hillsborough football ground tragedy in 1989, train crashes, plane crashes, terrorist atrocities – it would hit me harder than ever before. I could put myself in the place of those who lost loved ones, and feel it. I wrote this poem as I pondered these disasters, and thought of heaven.

A Matter of Death and Life

Disasters, death and devastation
What a painful age this is,
Train crashes, plane crashes
Earthquakes and fires,
How many victims this time?

The newscasters give us the numbers,
How important that seems to them.
How many dead? How many injured?
How many critically ill?
How many survived this time?

Sometimes there are no survivors,
No one comes out alive,
Hundreds gone – just like that
With no warning, no bedside prayers,
No time to say goodbye.

We have our personal disasters:
A son never arrives home from school;
A husband did not reach his work;
A mother knocked down in the street;
Then the number **one** is too much.

This life to us is so important,
We hang on to it, it's all we have;
But the thread it hangs on is fragile,
So easily broken - and then what?
That's what we need to know.

If our life here can end so abruptly,
We need to be ready for what's next.
It can't just end, and that's that!
All that we've had — that's the best?
There must be something more.

What if this life is just preparation
For what's in store for us when we die?
If we can build up lasting treasure
To take with us when we go,
There's meaning and purpose in life.

Then there's something to aim for,
Some reason for being here, being me;
Instead of just doing my best, then
In an instant I'm gone — it's all over,
Like a sandcastle washed away by the sea.

Well, is there some lasting treasure?
Is there something of me that goes on?
That will cross the death barrier with me
And be part of me forever, yes — me?
Is there anything of me that will last?

Faith, hope and love all endure,
(So the Bible would have us believe)
And the greatest of these is love.
Yes, love wins against all the odds,
The selfless love that comes from God.

God loves, he is love, that's who he is!
He cannot be anything else;
He created love, knowing full well
That love is the answer to all,
If only his world would believe.

And in the next life, there's love,
Such love that we've never known;
All communication is in love
So words are not really needed
As love is the language there!

So let's build up our treasure here,
A huge treasure trove of love;
And as it blesses people in this life
It's preparing our hearts too,
For the amazing destination above!

On THURSDAY MARCH 16ᵗʰ I had written:

I've been so upset since hearing on the news last night
that a vicar and his wife have lost their three daughters
in a fire, only their son was saved. Father, only you can
keep them from cracking up. Oh God, help them!

I couldn't bear to think about that loss and could only pray for them.

Then I had a dream and it was mixed up with Niki, but
somehow Niki came back to me, just for a day, and I
seemed to know that it was just for that time, after
which she 'died' again. But she was extraordinarily
radiant and beautiful, though in normal clothes. I was
sitting in a church hugging her, but nobody else seemed
to notice her. It was odd, but very lovely for me. I didn't
seem to mind her going back — well, of course I didn't
like it, but I knew she had to go back — she was
needed...

That was a special dream that God gave me, I think, to help me through at that time. It seemed to bless me, whereas most dreams about Niki left me upset afterwards, when it all became real again that she was gone. One in particular was awful when I dreamt of Niki being twelve years old and leaving home, and it was horrible. It lingered with me, until thankfully a friend rang me and my mood was lifted.

But even in this time of deep despair, there was still that longing in me to bring good out of this trauma.

MONDAY AUGUST 7th

> I want to use my time well; I want to be helpful to people, and fruitful. I want to help parents who lose their children, and others who are bereaved, yet I feel so helpless to do so.

I wanted to help others, but it was clearly too soon. I still had some way to go on my journey through the grief before I could reach out to help others.

THURSDAY AUGUST 10th

I wrote:

> The grief of losing Niki washes over us still, and brings us low when other pressures and problems crowd in too.

I read in the Bible: "Our days on earth are like grass, like wild flowers we bloom and die; the wind blows and we are gone, as if we had never been here."[37]

> That's how our life on earth is – like a flower blooming, then dying, and all around it goes on as it was. When Niki died, it seemed that everything should stop – how could everything around go on as if nothing had happened? But it does; life goes on now, and only last night I was thinking about this. It goes on, we get 'used' to living without Niki, and time goes on. But I still felt like stopping the world and getting off.

20

Acceptance and Readjustment

We were now into our third year without Niki, and it was going on for ever. That was so hard to think about, that the rest of our lives here would be without her.

For some time, I fought against this "new ground," this new family unit – just two children, with an age gap of six years. I have just one brother who is nine years older than me, and I always wanted three children, close together in age. I really enjoyed having my three, with two or three years between each of them, and after Niki's death I desperately wanted to fill the void. I thought about child-minding, fostering, or adopting; as long as it was a girl of an age between my two sons. But it doesn't work like that, and I knew deep down that nothing could fill that gap. Nothing and no-one will ever fill that gap, but as Ingrid Trobisch wrote:

> [God] has made a bridge over it. I can live with it now and I can stand on this bridge and reach out to others.[1]

I found comfort in thinking about Niki being in heaven. I came across a small notebook in which I used to write down what I was praying for family and friends, and realised that my prayers for Niki had been answered, though not in the way I expected or wished for.

Early in 1987 I had been praying for Niki to have more of a gentle spirit. It was there deep down, but things like impatience and a quick temper would take over a lot of the time. After her death, I wrote that she now has that gentle spirit, without the other things getting in the way. There are no bad things in heaven. I had also been praying for her to know Jesus better. She had given her life to Jesus at a Christian camp we all went to the year before, and loved singing about him

---

[1] Ingrid Trobisch, *Learning to Walk Alone* (Bolivar, MO: Quiet Waters, 2002). Quoted by kind permission.

and praying in her own way, making up her own songs to him. Now she is really close to him, something so special I can't imagine it. I envy you, Niki! I had also been praying for her bad dreams to stop. Now she has no bad dreams! I prayed about her friends – now she has innumerable friends. There is such love around her.

But we were left in this life, and in order to come through the grieving, we had to leave Niki behind, let go of her, while at the same time never wanting to forget her. As time went on, we had to get used to being family without her. It's like being pulled in opposite directions, it's hard to explain. We wanted to keep her close, remember what her voice sounded like and keep imagining her with us. Yet because life goes on, we have to get on with our lives without her, and some memories – like the sound of her voice – get fainter. While we keep longing for her to come back, we are still mourning, and the pain is too much. We can't live with that pain there all the time.

I'm talking about years now, not months. It was about two years before I could tell people "My daughter has died," without feeling deep pain or saying to myself, "No, it can't be true."

This final stage of grief, as the bereaved person gradually comes to terms with the death, is about accepting it as a fact and readjusting their daily life accordingly. A sign of this stage is when the one who is bereaved can talk about the person who has died without being overwhelmed by the sorrow. I remember Steve walking home from school on his birthday later in his teens and getting caught in a sudden thunderstorm. He laughed to himself as he imagined it was from Niki, a way of wishing him a happy birthday! He was able to think of her in fun ways, a sign of healing taking place.

Part of the process of making real to us what had happened was having a gravestone erected on Niki's grave. It's something you never imagine – what you would write on your child's gravestone.

It took us some time to think about, but eventually we were ready.

There was a lovely old man local to the cemetery who did "Ecclesiastic & Monumental Restorations, Conservation and Gilding." It sounds very grand! He did it all in a workshop on a farm. The inscription reads:

TREASURE IN HEAVEN
NICOLA JOY GATTING
8 Oct 1977 – 10 June 1987
"A little flower, lent not given
To bud on earth, but bloom in heaven"
See you there Niki!

That spoke from our hearts. We had loved having Nicola Joy to look after, to see her come into bud. Now we had to let her go, to flower in that place called heaven, which had become all the more real to us now. We have the assurance that one day we will see her there, and she will be showing us around. She always did want to be first, in everything!

Although we were letting go, I learnt to take time on the special anniversaries, especially her birthday, to immerse myself in memories of Niki. I used it as a special time. There was always something that was a real blessing on those days. In the weeks after Niki died, her Sunday school teacher, a lovely woman, gave us a gift of a rosebush to plant in Niki's memory. I think she had done the same in memory of her husband, who had died some years earlier. Thankfully my dad was a keen gardener so he took care of planting it for us in our front garden. We were amazed and delighted when it flowered the following year with pink roses for the anniversary of Niki's death in June, and again in October for her birthday! It was like a gift from Niki, something beautiful to warm our hearts when we felt so sad. I can say now, after thirty years, that it still bears roses around those anniversaries. What a wonderful gift that has been!

I remember on one of those anniversaries driving the twenty-five miles to the cemetery on my own, and in drizzly rain, in my sandals and no coat, I made two identical floral arrangements with silk flowers. There were bright pink carnations, deep blue iris, and tiny white daisies. I knew Niki would like the colours, and I felt really good creating them. I left one on her grave and brought the other one home so that I could enjoy looking at it as I thought of Niki.

That was a "mum" thing, not something the rest of the family necessarily appreciated. We all went bowling that evening, followed by some pizza. Usually when her birthday came round each year we would celebrate it as a family by doing something special, like going to the theatre, or having a trip out. We mixed the sadness with some fun, imagining Niki enjoying it with us, until the boys got older and it petered out. We still ring that date on the calendar, though. It will never go away.

This is a poem sent to me when Niki died:

A Child Loaned

"I'll lend you for a little time
A child of mine," He said,
"For you to love her while she lives
And mourn for when she's dead.
It may be six or seven years
Or twenty-two or three,
But will you, till I call her back,
Take care of her for me?
She'll bring her charms to gladden you
And should her stay be brief,
You'll have her lovely memories
As solace for your grief.

I cannot promise she will stay
Since all from earth return,
But there are lessons taught down there
I want this child to learn.
I've looked this wide world over
In my search for teachers true,
And from the throngs that crowd life's lanes
I have selected you.
Now will you give her all your love,
Not think the labour vain,

Nor hate me when I come to call
And take her back again?"

I fancied that I heard them say,
"Dear Lord, your will be done;
For all the joy your child shall bring
The risk of grief we'll run.
We'll shelter her with tenderness,
We'll love her while we may,
And for the happiness we've known
For ever grateful stay;
But should the angels call for her
Much sooner than we planned,
We'll brave the bitter grief that comes
And try to understand".[2]

---

[2] Edgar Albert Guest, first published in a newspaper circa 1930, reprinted in *Living The Years* 1949 publ. Chicago, Reilly & Lee Co. I have changed "he" to "she."

21

Looking Outwards

A big part of the healing process for me was to be able to help other grieving parents. I felt strongly that if God had allowed this to happen to us, then it must be for a purpose, and it must be put to good use. I sensed that I was now in a unique position to come alongside other bereaved parents, because I was one of them now. I had earned the right to say, "I know something of what you are feeling. I know what it's like to see your child die." It was a club that no one would want to join, but when you find yourself in it, you want to stick together. You want to cry with each other, and give each other help and support.

It says in the Bible: "God is the source of all comfort. He comforts us in all our troubles so that we can comfort others. When they are troubled, we will be able to give them the same comfort God has given us."[33]

Passing on the help we had received to others was, for me, part of the way God was going to bring good out of the terrible tragedy we had experienced. Remember God's promise in the Bible: "All things work together for good, for those that love God."[12]

THURSDAY MAY 18th 1989

I wrote, after reading in the Bible how Jesus healed a little girl:

Jesus could have healed Niki like that, and it would have brought great glory to God; but people soon forget, or water it down. There must be more glory to come from Niki's death, somehow, and I find that exciting. Have your way, Lord, and please use our tragedy and pain for good.

MONDAY AUGUST 7th

I want to use the hard times, the lean years we've experienced, by helping others through such times — to give them the help and encouragement that we have longed for so much.

I knew one or two other couples who had each lost a child, and it helped to be able to share with them, and know that they understood. I now wanted to prepare to give help to other bereaved parents. Because of my tragedy and suffering, I had a sensitivity to others that I did not have before, and I wanted to put that to good use.

In the autumn of 1989, I found an evening class locally doing a course on bereavement counselling. It was run by the diocese. I felt ready for this now, and it seemed to be what I was looking for, so I signed up for it and started attending. I can't remember much about it, except that it was a small group, and quite informal, as we learnt and shared experiences together. It was probably part of my moving on in the grieving process, as well as learning about how to help others through bereavement.

After completing the course, I contacted The Compassionate Friends, a charity of bereaved parents and families that supports other parents and their families who have suffered the death of a child. I hadn't contacted them before, for help, not really knowing about them at first, and then not brave enough to go to a group several miles away, not knowing anyone. Now I thought I could join a group and help in some way. However, I didn't hear back, I don't know why, so I looked for another avenue.

There was a branch nearby of Cruse Bereavement Care, so I contacted them so see what I could do. I was interviewed by the Chairman, who accepted my training (from the evening class) and took me on as a counsellor.

MONDAY MAY 21st 1990

The Cruse meeting on Saturday was good – I felt so at home with the other people, so right to be there. I have my first client to ring today – a Mum whose 6yr old daughter died last summer.

As Cruse counsellors, we visited clients in their homes. As I set out to visit my first client, it felt like a baptism of fire! I felt completely inadequate, but was trusting God to help me be what I needed to be for her.

It's etched in my memory, that first session. She had the television on while she was ironing, and just carried on with it, as I sat there. She was too tearful to speak.

Her daughter had died of leukaemia. She had watched her gradually get weaker and weaker. She was devastated, of course, and I thought, "What on earth can I do to help her?"

After a few moments of silence, I decided to take a chance and do something you must be very wary of in counselling – I told her briefly about my own bereavement, the death of my daughter.

Having shared briefly, my client then started asking *me* questions about *my* daughter's death. This was the wrong way round, and I felt I was doing it all wrong. The teaching I'd been given was to listen, reflect back, and show empathy.

Well, we ended up both being tearful, so I think she felt the empathy, and was able to start telling her story. It opened things up, but I felt guilty going back to my supervisor. He asked how I got on, and I told him, hesitantly, what I had done. He smiled, and said it was fine; it was great, in fact, because it so clearly helped her to verbalise what was on her heart. Our sessions went better after that.

I read later in some bereavement training notes: "Self-disclosure, revealing information about oneself, needs to be used carefully when counselling, and be similar in tone and expression to what the client is expressing or experiencing. When used appropriately it may be helpful in showing empathy and increase the ability of the client to talk about their own grief." I had done just that, and it had really helped.

Bereavement counselling is about helping the person to make real what has happened to them – something they don't want to do. So it needs a lot of time, a lot of listening and showing that you understand. It's not counselling to help them get better again, back to where they felt alright, because they can't, it's not possible. It's about helping them get to a point where they accept what has happened to them and start to move on into the next part of their life.

When I say listening is required, I mean quality listening. When have you tried to tell someone about a painful or distressing experience, only to have them interrupt you, before you have finished, with a monologue about a bad experience they have had? It's painful! It feels like someone has trodden on you. The focus has gone from you to them as they have not allowed you to talk about your own experience. You don't feel that the listener cares about you at all.

Listening is such a valuable tool in helping troubled people. It sounds simple, but is far from it. It means listening carefully, observantly, feelingly, and discerningly. It means showing by your body language that you care, e.g. not sitting back with your arms crossed and a bored expression on your face. That may be an extreme example, but I'm sure you understand what I am saying. It means reading the body language of the other person. Did you know that in communication, the three main elements are; words, body language, and tone of voice? The smallest of those is words, not more than 10%, whilst the greatest is body language, more than 50%.

So listening, and reflecting back – what does that mean? The counsellor needs to be able to summarise key thoughts and feelings, and express them back to show that the person is heard and understood.

And the counsellor needs to show empathy. Empathy is being able to understand how another person is feeling, feeling what it's like in their shoes whilst firmly standing in one's own. Sympathy is more detached – feeling sorry for someone without understanding the feelings and experience.

Empathy means staying with the feelings but keeping an objective outlook, in order to sort through the emotionally expressed information without being overcome by it. It helps to have experienced something similar, but it's not essential.

Let me give you another example of how this worked in practice.

I visited Jane (not her real name) regularly as her bereavement counsellor from three months after the death of her son until the time of the first anniversary. Her teenage son had been inhaling aerosols with another boy when he had collapsed, hallucinating, and died within minutes. Jane had been told by a policeman knocking at her door. What a terrible tragedy.

I visited weekly to start with, and those first few weeks consisted of Jane talking over and over the events of the death, the shock of it, and how she could not believe she would never see her son again. She was reliving the experience every Saturday evening still, as that was when it happened.

Something that was difficult for me in those first visits was that the TV was always on, as with my first client, and left on throughout the hour or so that I was there. This was potentially distracting for me in my listening, but I recognised that Jane would be uneasy with silence. As a counsellor, I was trained to allow silence, as it is often needed for the client to control their tears, or collect their thoughts, but it's not easy for someone in an emotional state to sit in silence with a stranger.

After two or three visits, the sound was turned right down. As long as I sat where I could not see it, I could really concentrate on Jane. Eventually she felt at ease enough to turn it off, which was a really encouraging sign of progress.

After a few weeks, Jane told me tentatively that she had been to a medium to try to find out if her son was "alright." The medium had told her things about him that she could not have known, that were not in the press reports, and Jane was comforted to hear that he was happy now. She asked my views on this – a difficult one for me to answer, as in working for a non-religious organisation, I could not put on her my own beliefs. However, as she had already revealed that she went to a Roman Catholic Church, I felt free to say that the Bible warns against this, and that her priest would probably agree that it was not a good idea. She did not plan to revisit the medium, but if she had I would have gently tried to tell her that getting through our grief means coming to a point where we stop trying to "find" the one that has died. We accept the reality of the death. I also encouraged her to talk to her priest about her son so that she could consolidate what she believed about life after death.

Jane needed to express more than once her "if only" feelings about what had happened to her son. She had been away on a course for work the week leading up to his death, only returning home on the Friday evening. She kept thinking that if only she had been home that week she might have noticed a clue to him inhaling aerosols, perhaps some unusual behaviour. It was thought after the post mortem that he had only done this once or twice. In talking this through, she convinced herself that if there had been anything to notice, her daughter would have seen it, as the siblings were quite close. Also, as a typical mother of teenagers, she would not have gone prying into his room. Even after his death she felt guilty going through his things, as a teenager likes his privacy.

Jane also had feelings to express about the boy her son was with, who had apparently been inhaling for some time, and was still alive. Where is the justice in this? Perhaps if they had moved away before, as she had wanted to, this would not have happened? If only. This stage seems to be a necessary one to go through, and can be really distressing for the bereaved person, but if expressed it does pass. Jane came to accept that nothing could change what had happened.

As time went on, I was able to encourage Jane to talk about good memories of her son – how he got on at school and how he helped elderly neighbours – something she did not know about until they told her after his death. These little things brought comfort, as did the memorials that the school arranged.

She was also concerned about her daughter, who was obviously grieving, but would not often talk about her brother. I could understand that concern, as we had felt that about our son Steve. I suggested that maybe she was talking more to her friends about him, and without pushing her she would probably open up to Jane in her own time. That had been my experience with Steve, and it turned out to be the same for Jane with her daughter. We all grieve in different ways, at different times, and need to walk through it as we are able.

I had let Jane know at some point that I had lost a child, and at times she would ask "Did you feel like that?" When I replied positively, it seemed like a weight lifted off her shoulders. For instance, when she talked about her daughter. She was afraid to let her out of her sight for long, after the death. I was able to share with her the fear of siblings that someone else in the family is going to die. This fear slowly fades. All that I learned through my tragic experience added to the training I received, and if used wisely I found it could be of great comfort to the client.

As the months went on, I encouraged Jane to gradually sort out her son's room, so that when the time came for her planned move it would not be an overwhelming task. It was satisfying to see her moving on in her grief, and to prepare her for her son's birthday, and the first anniversary, which unfortunately were within weeks of each other. Before I finished seeing her, she was meeting in a group at her church, set up by the supportive priest, for people with deep needs. She told me how she came alongside a woman whose child had recently been run over and killed, and was able to start passing on the help and comfort she herself had received.

What a pleasing ending! We didn't always get to see our clients moving on so positively. It greatly increased my confidence, as I realised how much help can be given by just listening with compassion and understanding. I also learnt not to be perturbed by distractions, but to go with them and let them work themselves out. If I was at ease in any situation, then the client would eventually relax too. It often seemed like I had done nothing really, except listen, yet the client would be so grateful for the help.

22

The Compassionate Friends

I continued throughout 1990, doing bereavement counselling with Cruse Bereavement Care. Then one Sunday evening early in 1991 I had an unexpected call from The Compassionate Friends. It came as a great surprise, as I had forgotten about my query a year previously. I don't know what happened in the meantime as far as they were concerned, but suddenly I was being invited to go to a meeting in St. John's Wood, London.

Dave came with me to support, as I duly went to the meeting on March 4th. Most of the business was talking about the Central London group, which really needed to be divided up into the appropriate areas, if there were the personnel available. I felt very strongly that I should start a group in West London, with another lady there from my area, whom I'll call Jill. I felt quite excited about the prospect.

Looking back, I could see that I was then in a better place to start a group, having had experience doing bereavement counselling. I wondered if God hid my letter to them for a year, until I was ready! The Compassionate Friends (TCF) does not offer counselling, but friendship and understanding to other bereaved parents. The only necessary qualification was that I was one myself.

Two days later Jill rang me about TCF and we talked about starting a group.

WEDNESDAY MARCH 6th

> God seems to be moving me on fast – I can feel the momentum. We must stop to consider the pitfalls, we said, before we actually start, e.g. one person monopolising the group meeting? Jill's coming over on Friday morning with names and addresses of people to start with.

Things accelerated.

TUESDAY MARCH 19th

While I was out this evening Dave took a call for me from T. at TCF, asking if I would go on a phone-in - at the BBC! He was so shocked he hadn't taken her telephone number — good job I had it! I rang her back and discovered it's a Helpline after a program "Family Matters" on Monday at 7:30 p.m. About 6 of us going. I'll be there till about 11:00 p.m.

WEDNESDAY MARCH 20th

I'm excited about God moving on my bereavement work — it's happening so fast now!

It was quite an experience going to the BBC Television Centre, and after the program I had the opportunity to answer two or three calls. It was not so easy listening on a phone line, but I did my best and trust it was a help to the callers.

Jill and I set about publicising our first meeting of TCF – we put posters up in libraries and doctor's surgeries. We were also given names by TCF of those in our area who had called them for help at some point. I also contacted the local Gazette who had carried our story of Niki's death. They were very keen to do an article about our plans. It was a long article, going through how Niki died again. This is some of what it said:

A Pain so Deep Cannot Last Forever
(Acton Gazette, FRIDAY April 26, 1991)

A couple whose nine-year-old daughter died in a million-to-one tragedy, days after breaking her wrist in a playground accident, are to help set up a friendship group for bereaved parents.

Ruth and Dave Gatting ... want to help other mums and dads overcome the enormous grief suffered when a child dies. With the help of another bereaved mother the couple are to set up the first Ealing Branch of The Compassionate Friends.

Ruth and Dave's only daughter, Nicola, who would have been 13 this year, died in 1987....

A coroner's report described her death as a million-to-one tragedy.

Four years after Nicola was buried her parents are setting up the only West London branch of TCF.

Ruth said: "It took me two years before I could tell people 'My daughter is dead,' without feeling pain or saying to myself, 'No, it can't be true.'"

And she says she was one of the lucky people who had love and support whichever way she turned.

"The warmth and support I got from friends I knew through her school, from the church and neighbours was tremendous. I was scared stiff of going back into the school playground but if the other mothers did not know what to say to me they just gave me a hug. The affection was overwhelming, wonderful."

Ruth wrote to TCF and became involved with Ealing Cruse, another organisation which offers help to the bereaved. The new branch, which will hold its first meeting on Monday, May 13th will meet in Ruth and Dave's home once a month.

Parents who have just lost their child or children and those who are still learning to live with the loss after months or years are welcome. At meetings parents will be given a chance to talk in small groups and they will be encouraged to remember their child.

Ruth and Dave, who have two boys, 16 and 9, always celebrate Nicola's birthday and do something she would have enjoyed. Ruth said, "We talk about her all the time. She is still part of the family...."

Nicola is remembered at her former school every day. There is a bench in the playground paying tribute to her. But this lovely little girl lives on in the hearts and minds of all those who knew her, Ruth says.

She added: "Even now I hear little tales of things she did and said. Some good comes from grief and suffering. If our experiences can help people to realise that the sorrow does not go on for ever, then that is a good thing."

On the whole, it was a good article, even if not exactly as I would express it all, and now there was no turning back. Our names, address and telephone numbers were out there – scary! I'm not sure I would be so brave now, but I was really fired up at that time, and raring to go.

THURSDAY MAY 9th

Jill round this evening to finalise things for Monday, CF group. I have 12 names, Jill has 3 – quite a crowd. Dave helping with organisation but otherwise I seem to hold the reins. Jill is keeping herself as deputy, I feel, but I'm ok!

Two days later I was doing a training day with Cruse on telephone skills. That would prove to be very useful, as being a TCF group leader meant I was a contact that anyone could ring, day or night, for help with their grief.

MONDAY MAY 13th

Mad clean and tidy up all day! Not time to be nervous – just started panicking about 6:30 p.m. and then Dave walked in – great!

People a bit awkward for first hour, but by 9:30 p.m. everyone was relaxed and mingling (in a cramped way!)

We had the help and support of the National Development Co-ordinator for TCF at that first meeting, which was a blessing. We had eleven bereaved parents there that evening: a couple whose teenage son had been stabbed; a mother whose adult son died at Hillsborough; a mother whose disabled son died aged twenty; a father whose teenage son was found dead in his bed; a mother whose daughter, twenty-one, had choked; a mother whose five-year-old daughter died of cancer; a mother whose adult son committed suicide; a mother whose teenage daughter took an overdose; a mother whose teenage daughter died in a road traffic accident; and a mother whose adult son died from an asthma attack.

All that tragedy and grief in one place.

What can I say? Such lovely people, such traumatic, sad stories – but we had a common link and as we shared our stories we felt such empathy for each other.

I laid out our aims as a group:

- To help each other through the grief of losing a child.
- To encourage the working through of that grief, to eventually come to terms with the loss, facing feelings and expressing them.
- To do this by providing a warm, compassionate environment where it is safe to express our feelings, to cry if we want to, without fear of being judged or criticised.
- To be able to talk in small groups with kindred spirits, without feeling threatened or overwhelmed.
- For those of us who have crossed some of the hurdles to help those who are more recently bereaved to work through some of the practical problems.

Our hidden aims, as leaders, were:

- To get members helping one another, outside of the meeting.
- Ultimately some to help in or run groups.
- To come to the point where they don't need the group and become self-reliant.

The TCF group was not meant to become a permanent fixture in the lives of the bereaved parents. To be healthy, it needed to move people on.

Some people we contacted didn't feel comfortable coming to a group meeting, as I hadn't in the first year or two of bereavement. I felt for them, and visited or spoke to them on the phone instead.

As I began to take calls from newly bereaved parents, usually mothers, I had to be careful to look after myself, as it could be really draining. They always wanted to hear my story. They needed to know that I knew what it was like to lose a child. I took opportunities to meet with those who supported me, including a mum whose son had died some time before Niki, who was further along the grieving road. That felt like input for me, to balance what I was giving out to TCF.

I also got more training from Cruse. I remember going to Brighton for the day for a training day on group work, which was very useful.

MONDAY JUNE 24th

Second TCF meeting

Nine of us this evening, but good to be in one group, and had quite a bit of whole group discussion. Comments showed that they felt relaxed, easy to talk. One lady told Dave I was wonderful, a really good listener – what a compliment.

As the meetings went on each month, there was often some sharing in twos and threes at the beginning, but we tried to have some group discussions on topics that affected us all. These were on subjects like coping with Christmas and the birthdays of our children no longer with us; how to deal with our child's possessions; how we cope with unhelpful comments from acquaintances.

Other concerns were unique to individuals:

- A court case after a road accident or deliberate killing.
- Nursing a sick child with a terminal illness.
- The shock of a sudden death, including suicide.
- Public disaster followed by TV and press coverage.
- Coping with the death of a disabled child.
- The death of an only child and loss of parental role.
- Trying to help our surviving children in their grief.
- Maintaining a relationship with grandchildren after the death of one of their parents.

I continued counselling with Cruse, in tandem with The Compassionate Friends. Of the two, the work with TCF was more draining, as I could get a call from a bereaved parent at any time on our home phone line. In those days I didn't know, till I answered it, who was ringing. Steve told me that he could tell when it was a TCF call as my tone of voice changed, as I moved into compassionate listening mode. What helped them so much was someone who had been through a similar experience now listening to their story.

Bereavement counselling was not so wearing, as I knew something about the person I was seeing, and it was a complete focus on that person and his or her needs. I was also in control of the time spent listening, usually no more than an hour. My bereavement helped me to understand, but it was generally not something the other person knew about.

So there came a time, after a few years, when I felt I needed to let go of the work with TCF. The group had dwindled a bit by then, and those who came regularly were able to support each other in an informal manner outside of the meetings. Others had come and gone, using it for a few months to help them along then they had moved on.

I kept up my work with Cruse, and at the beginning of 1991, I became a supervisor, overseeing a group of counsellors and making sure of their wellbeing as they did a good work, whilst being a step away from seeing bereaved people myself.

23

The Year of the Killer Bug Scare

Towards the end of May 1994, something came up in the news which really impacted me and threw me back into the whole scenario surrounding Niki's death.

The front pages of the newspapers each day carried headlines like:

Chilling Times in the Village of the Killer Bug
(Evening Standard TUESDAY MAY 24th 1994)

Now Bug Kills Young Mother
(Daily Mail WEDNESDAY MAY 25th 1994)

More Victims of Killer Bug
(Daily Mail THURSDAY MAY 26th 1994)

What was going on? People were dying after simple accidents or minor operations, or after just finding a rash on their skin, or a lump. They were dying within days, and the common factor present in their bodies was streptococcus A, the bacteria that causes sore throats.

This sounded so familiar. Their flesh was getting eaten away like gangrene. The diagnosis was necrotising fasciitis. The paper WEDNESDAY MAY 25th 1994 read:

> Microbiologists are trying to discover exactly why and how the "galloping gangrene" bug develops. It is triggered by the comparatively common streptococcus bacteria, which normally causes minor infections such as sore throats. Scientists believe necrotising fasciitis may be the result of a virus latching on to the bacteria.

Apparently, it was usually the cause of two or three deaths a year in Britain. By 25th May 1994, the number had risen to twelve deaths already that year. The latest was a twenty-eight-year-old woman, infected days after giving birth. Surgeons removed dead flesh from her abdomen and treated her with strong antibiotics as she lay critically ill in the intensive care unit. She appeared to improve and was ready to leave hospital about ten days later when her condition suddenly worsened and she died.

Some survived after having the infected flesh removed. One died after having a leg amputated.

Medical officers tried to calm the public. I was not afraid – my daughter had died already, several years before – but it made me think, and wonder if this was the cause of her death? Would it help to answer the questions of how and why she died?

I contacted the consultant paediatrician who had treated Niki and asked him about it. He was very understanding and made an appointment for me to go and talk it through with him. I went to see him in July. He was very sweet; he hadn't realised that it was so long – seven years – since Nicola's death. I was amazed he remembered her.

He looked through all the records of the investigations which were carried out at the time of Niki's final illness and said there was no doubt that the organism (group A streptococcus) which was isolated in her was of the same species which had been incriminated in the recently publicised cases. So, it looked as if this was the cause of Niki's death – necrotising fasciitis.

I can't say it made a big difference to me, but somehow it was good to know there was a name for what happened to Niki. Perhaps now I could just say – when people asked how she died – that she had necrotising fasciitis, as one would say "leukaemia," for instance. It would be helpful not to have to tell the whole complicated story when people asked. But actually, when I did give the name, the one asking usually had no idea what it was, so I still had to explain the details.

24

The Impact on Our Lives

Our tragedy changed each of us in the family. We became more sensitive about each other's needs and feelings, and I believe we still are. We are very close as a family, even though Steve and Paul are now adult men and living away from home. In fact, Steve, who found it so hard to go away from home after his experience with Niki's death while he was on a school trip, is now living and working in America! They are loving, caring, kind and thoughtful young men, and we are very proud of them.

As I write this, thirty years later, I realise again how my experience has sensitised me to the grief of others in similar circumstances. In the news today is the agony of a mother who lost her only little son, one year old, when it could – it turns out – have been prevented. If only doctors had seen the signs of sepsis instead of continually saying over several appointments that it was just a cold or asthma. Her little boy was not getting better, he was getting worse, and she kept asking the medical profession for help. I want them to realise that a mother knows her child; she knows when something is not right. It reminds me of the young doctor that told me not to fuss, saying Niki would be fine. We mothers devote ourselves to keeping our child happy and well. We sense when something is seriously wrong, and doctors need to recognise that.

Dave and I both came through our tragedy with a deeper sensitivity to others, being much more aware of the feelings and needs of those going through difficult times. It set us on a path we hadn't previously considered.

My perspective on life changed noticeably. I had never been especially materialistic, but things like my home and my possessions were important to me. After losing my little girl, it was like having part of me wrenched away; material things were suddenly trivial, irrelevant by comparison. If we lost something, or if something got spilt on the carpet or furniture

– so what? What did it matter? Yes, we cleaned up, we maintained the home, but it was not something to get upset about, not at all. It was each other in the family, our health and well-being that was important. Things can be replaced, but not people whom we love.

Going through such a terrible tragedy, and making steady improvement through the grieving process made me a stronger, more confident person. I could hold my head up high because I had made it through such a traumatic experience. I will always be a bereaved mum, but I have made it part of my life. It's who I am, but I can move on as I make it part of the new me. I used to be a person who liked quick results and was not very good at waiting for things or working through situations that were hard and needed perseverance. But it takes courage and endurance to work through deep grief – there is no way round it – and it changed me for the better. I have learnt to work through difficult situations with more patience and understanding.

Before Niki died I would probably have avoided people who were in deep sadness, feeling awkward and not knowing what to say. Afterwards I was drawn to them as my heart went out to them in their grief. I'd experienced a huge trauma and I wanted to use it to help others. There was also a deep sense that I had earned the right to come alongside the grieving and bereft because of my own tragic loss. I could walk with them, having some awareness of what they were going through.

As time went on, I felt I was progressing into giving people more varied pastoral care, in a church situation primarily, and needed some training to do it properly. I also thought I might move into general counselling, not focussing on helping bereaved people all the time. With bereavement counselling, there is not a problem to be fixed to get the person back to where they were before. They will never be the same again. I wanted to be a positive help in individuals' lives, to help them overcome something that was stopping them from functioning in what was the normal way for them.

So in 1993, I did a Pastoral Care correspondence course with a college in Nottingham, going up there for two short spells of in house training as part of that. It was a very good experience and helped me a lot. I then did a year's Christian counselling course locally, and later Dave also did some counselling training.

We moved into counselling, sometimes seeing a client together, sometimes separately. On the whole, we worked well together, even though we are very different. Dave was good at remembering the facts and details that the client shared with us, and I would pick up the emotions behind the words. Coming through the whole experience of losing Niki had deposited in me a natural sensitivity to people's feelings, so that is what I noticed as they would tell their story. I was then able to feed back to them what I was sensing, and help them through it to a place where they were more able to move on with their lives.

As I continued counselling, it required regular sessions with a supervisor, to make sure I was doing my job properly, and that I was in a good and healthy place in it. It was necessary to keep notes on every session, and have ongoing training. After a few years, I was finding this hard work, and I began to feel my heart was not in it. It's not that my desire to help people waned, but I didn't like the formality of the counselling set-up. I began to feel relief when a client rang to cancel an appointment for some reason – not a good sign! I also liked to pray with people after listening to them, something which didn't necessarily fit into the normal counselling session.

My heart was, and still is, to come alongside individuals who are struggling with life issues. Dave and I both long to see people grow into their full potential and mature in their faith.

Going through the dark time of bereavement made me much more aware of God in my life, and how he sees everything about us and is interested in every detail of our lives. Since then it's been my heart to pass that on to others, so that when they are going through hard times they too can know that help.

I have become like a spiritual mum to some younger women. I love to have one-to-one time with female friends, over coffee or lunch, listening to where they are in their lives, showing them God's love and bringing encouragement where I can. I also love to pray with and for individuals, to see them progess in all that God has for them, and have done that over the years in churches and other Christian organisations.

In a church environment, Dave and I have also had responsibility for pastoring leaders of small groups, making sure of their well-being as they carried out their leadership roles. Pastoring seems to come naturally to us, as that is how our hearts have developed over the years.

Dave and I also moved into running training courses, something Dave really loves doing. We were teaching others how to help, particularly how to help the bereaved, and how to give individuals quality listening time. We ran training courses for church groups and for a local council group. This is very much Dave's gifting, not so much mine, but I did my bit for a few years until I decided it was not really my forté. We also shared our insights of heaven to some groups, as the reality of it had impacted us strongly, needing to know where Niki is now. We wanted to inspire others with that hope.

So as the years have passed, we have continued to grow in sensitivity, and have sought to help all those whom God has put in front of us, drawing on the strength with which he continues to infuse us. He is our Rock, and always will be, and is completely trustworthy and faithful. We want to give him all the glory!

25

Revisiting the Black Forest

This book has revisited many of our memories of Niki – some painful, traumatic, and sad memories. But before finishing the story I wanted to end by revisiting some of the final good memories we made with Niki. This book started with the fun we had in The Black Forest, and I want it to end with those memories.

As part of the process, it felt important to go back there, to the geographical area, The Black Forest, and see if we could find some of the places we went to in 1987. This idea started after a visit to Berlin. We went there to see a special friend, Brigitte. Our visit to see her started us thinking of the link with Niki. It was four months after Niki died, that Brigitte came from Germany to London to live and work. Some years later, after meeting her through our church and getting to know her, she became integrated into our family, like an older sister to Steve and Paul. We started thinking of our holiday in Germany in May–June 1987. Perhaps we should revisit the place, and the memories?

So, Dave and I made plans, and at the end of May 2016, we flew to Basel to spend five days in the area around Freiburg. It wasn't until we were on our way that I realised, and commented to Dave, that we were going there around the same time of year as in 1987. This had not been deliberate; in fact, it had only just dawned on me. It was a busy time with comings and goings in the family, and other commitments, and that was the only week we felt we could fit in the trip. It was even half-term for schools, so probably more expensive than at other times, but I was determined to do it so off we went. It felt as if it could be really emotional, and we had no idea what to expect.

We landed at Basel Airport about 1:00 p.m. It's a confusing place, as half is in France and half in Switzerland. When we were booking the rental car online, we were not sure which part of the airport we wanted to be in to collect the car, but ended up having to collect it in the Swiss zone. That's where we hit a problem.

The rental car agent was very pleasant, and said that we could take the Swiss car we had ordered into Germany, but only if we first signed an agreement that we were totally responsible and liable for any damage to the car. What? Apparently, the EU had issued a new law on May 1st – no rental car with Swiss registration was allowed in EU countries!

So, what could we do? We asked her to transfer our booking to the same company in the French zone – but no, that was not possible. They were a separate Swiss franchise with no link with their French counterpart. Great!

So then ensued a long battle on the phone – to cancel our original booking, which eventually was done, so that we could start again and hire another car. To do that, we had to go up the stairs, along the corridor, and down the stairs again to reach the French part of the airport. We made our way to the same rental company, told them our problem. Could we hire a car please? The answer was no – they had none left at that time. Eventually we managed to hire a car from another company, getting an upgraded car because a mistake was made along the way.

This was not a promising start to our nostalgic adventure – was it all going to be as frustrating and problematic as this?

But hey! The sun was shining, and we set off on the next phase of our journey with renewed optimism!

With GPS, we found our way easily to our small family hotel, in a village amongst the mountains. In 1987, we drove all the way from Calais with just maps – no satellite navigation in those days. How did we do it, with three children in the back of the car too?

It was a hotel typical of the area, with balconies, window boxes and traditional dark furniture, beautifully maintained. When we checked in at reception, we were told we had a suite, wow! We felt really spoilt. The staff were friendly and helpful, and we had a lovely meal that evening and began to relax. It started us off on such a good note for this sentimental journey we were on. I felt God was definitely in this with us, giving us his peace.

We went down for breakfast the next morning, and were shown to a table with a tiny blackboard on it saying "Wilkommen Family Gatting." It was like we were there with our family! There was also a small pot on the table containing a single flower and a silk butterfly. I was so touched by that – the welcome to us, and the butterfly, which I always associate with Niki. That's since God gave me that poem about a caterpillar transforming into a butterfly, just like Niki going to heaven. Thank you, Lord – that is such a lovely sign for me here. You are a step ahead of me all the time.

WEDNESDAY JUNE 1st

Our first stop was the local Tourist Office, and the two young women there were very helpful and chatty; one, having been to London just a few weeks before, was delighted to speak English for some more practice. We got the map we needed and started off to find Kirchzarten, where we camped last time we were here. We didn't want to raise our hopes, but deep down, we wanted to find the same campsite. We'd brought photos we had taken then of our children in different places, and one was just outside our tent, in front of a small wire fence with the mountains in the background.

We reached Kirchzarten and were surprised it was quite a big town. Was it always like that, or had it grown a lot in all those years? Probably the latter! We drove right through it, thinking that the campsite must have been on the outskirts then, as there was the lovely mountain view from our tent. We started seeing signs to a campsite, and eagerly followed, until we came to Camping Kirchzarten. Yes!

There was a small car park nearby, so we parked there and wandered in, a bit cheekily, and started walking to the edge of the site, to where we thought our tent might have been. There were no tents to be seen now, just a huge site filled with caravans.

I had the photo in my hand, and suddenly, there it was. The same mountain, with the same distinctive tree pattern and clearings, away in the distance! There were some buildings in the way now, but we could just see the mountain we were looking for. However, it was not quite the same angle as in the photo, so we kept walking around the edge of the campsite, and suddenly found ourselves in an empty green area – the exact spot! There was even the same fence, or same kind of fence, in front of which the children were photographed. This was where we stayed, that last, fun-filled holiday with our three children. We turned around to see the space where the tent had been pitched, a dry patch on the grass. We tried to picture sitting outside as a family, eating our meals in the sunshine. We took lots of photos, to make sure we got a good one, with me posing where the children would have been.

For the rest of the day, I went around glowing. I kept smiling as I mulled over what we had discovered and the joy of sweet memories. We walked by a stream, with water wheels whirring round and had a scenic drive through the mountains. We sat in a café eating Black Forest gateau, then went for a drive round hairpin bends, up and up and up, getting cooler and cooler, then down again, back to 21 degrees centigrade. What a lovely day, finished off with a wonderful meal at our hotel with a glass or two of wine to celebrate our first victory!

THURSDAY JUNE 2nd

In 1987, this was the day we left the Black Forest, for one night at Luxembourg then home.

I felt a bit low as I woke, after not sleeping well for a second night. This was not unusual for me, but frustrating when I wanted to make the most of every day in this beautiful place without feeling tired and weary. I asked God for strength for the day, and read: "I watch in hope for the Lord, I wait for God my Saviour, my God will hear me."[38] Thank you, Lord.

The next item on our agenda was to find the toboggan run. In our search on the internet we had found several parks with toboggan runs in the area, so we narrowed it down to those that were nearest Kirchzarten. We had been looking at one park, and nearly decided to go there, when suddenly Dave found another one – Steinwasen Park. This one had a modern roller coaster ride, but what interested us was the older double bobsled run, exactly like the one in our photo of 1987. It hadn't registered with me that there were two parallel tracks back then, but it was there in our photos. There was a chairlift, and wildlife too, and we remembered seeing wild boars. This was definitely the one to try first.

It was a cloudy, cooler day, drizzly at times. As we drove past Kirchzarten and got nearer to Steinwasen Park, I had a déjà vu moment. Suddenly the road looked familiar, and I had a flashback to driving there as a family. I knew this was it! We paid our entry fee and entered the park. It advertises "The most spectacular alpine coaster of Germany!" but that was not what we were looking for. We were looking for an older toboggan run, and there it was.

The chairlift was there, the chairs going up and down, and as we glided peacefully upwards we could look down and see wild boars on the hillside, just as we remembered. We got to the top and saw where the toboggan run started. As we came back down in the chairlift we saw the view as it was in our photos from 1987 – the same lake, even some identical buildings, just a few more added. Absolutely amazing!

Later, we walked back up through the trees, where there were now more wild animals in big enclosures on the hillside – red deer, fallow deer, reindeer, ibex, chamois and European lynx.

After some lunch in the restaurant, Dave announced that he was going to ride down the toboggan run. "Really?" I said. "Are you sure?" I thought he was, well … a bit old to be doing such a thing. I definitely did NOT want to do it! He was adamant, wanting to relive that memory, and so I would be the photographer. I had just one chance to capture the moment for the photo album.

He reminded me that when we paid our entrance fee, the lady behind the desk had warned us that on the bobsled you are responsible for your own safety as you are in control of the brake. So, she expected us, at our age, to be using it. The written notice she gave us was funny, with the translation to English saying at the end: "We thank you for your understanding and now want much fun with the uses of the plants"! The German word "Anlagen" can be translated as industrial plants, as well as facilities, which it should have been, I think!

Before he took the plunge, we walked some way back up the hill to experience the rope suspension bridge, passing racoons and marmots, aviaries and donkeys, the latter roaming free. The rope bridge was the limit of my adventure this time. I have to be careful now as with osteoporosis, my travel insurance does not cover dangerous mountain sports!

Then I saw Dave off to take the chairlift uphill again to get the bobsled down. I got ready at my viewpoint, with my camera poised. I had to keep my stance, to get the shot. There was no way he would go down twice.

Suddenly there he was, careering down the run. He was hunched over, holding on to the stick which controlled the speed, with not much of a smile on his face. He said afterwards that it was really uncomfortable. And yes, I got my picture!

It seemed to give him a thirst for more, though. There was a newer rollercoaster ride, also with separate bobsleds which you could control, and he would have gone on it with me, if I was willing, which I definitely was not. Did something of Niki's adventurous spirit touch him? I didn't have the nerve without Niki there to egg me on.

The next day we caught the train into Freiburg, with free travel passes courtesy of Hotel Stollen. It was just a thirty-minute journey, and we could relax and not worry about car parking. One memory from 1987 was that we parked in an underground car park in Freiburg, and when we came to leave in the evening we had great difficulty understanding how to get out. That was scary!

We picked up a city map and started our tour, heading for the cathedral where Niki had insisted on climbing to the top of the tower. Now we wanted to do the same, in honour of our lovely daughter.

We went inside the cathedral, expecting to find steps there to go up to the top. It was very dark in there, and hard to find any sign of stairs, but after some inquiries we were directed to a door outside. There was a sign there which we didn't notice until we came out afterwards. It stated there were 209 steps. As we climbed up the steep spiral staircase, with very deep steps, it seemed never ending! Would we make it? We had to, once we started. We had to keep stopping for a rest, and sometimes had to squeeze in to let others pass on their way down. But we had to do it. We had to keep going. Eventually we puffed our way to what seemed like the top, where we had to pay two euros each for the privilege. We saw that it was not yet the highest point. There was an even narrower spiral staircase for the final bit, so I took time for a look around at the postcards and fridge magnets on sale – a good excuse for a breather.

When we reached the top, I had tentative looks down into the square below, which was bustling with market stalls. We had some photos with us of Niki and Steve in front of some beautiful buildings, and we'd seen one before starting our climb. Suddenly we saw the other one from our viewpoint. Exciting! Another memory to capture when we descended again. Going down was a lot easier. We got our photos of the buildings, though not so easy this time as the square was full of market stalls, not empty as it was all those years ago.

After all that exertion, we found a nice café in a small street, to sit outside and have some delicious gateau and a drink. Then we took time to do a walking tour of Freiburg, with Dave as the guide with a map in his hand – our own bit of adventure.

We had one more day left. Our last mission was to try to see a lake of which we had a photo. Niki had taken a photo of Dave and I at the top of a hill, with a beautiful lake down below in the valley. We had snow around our feet, but it was in bright sunshine.

Looking at a map, the only lake like that in the mountains was one called Feldsee, and Feldberg was the highest mountain, so probably the one we went up with our daughter who always wanted to go up as high as she could.

We got to the Feldberg area and had some pizza in a café, before going up in the cable car. The weather was a bit misty and drizzly, but it was now or never so we decided to go for it. Unfortunately, as we went up in the cable car the view disappeared, and we couldn't even see the car in front. At the top, we were completely in cloud, with no view at all.

This time our vision was blocked. We couldn't see everything we wanted to see.

It's like that with Niki. We can't see her now, we can't see how she is – we walk by faith.

We were fairly certain that from the top of Feldberg we should have been able to see Feldsee – it was there, the map said so.

We are one hundred percent certain that Niki is in heaven. God has given us the faith for that, and the vision in our imaginations. We trust our heavenly Father that one day the clouds will be lifted and we will see her again, as she meets us in heaven.

If there was something to climb, Niki always wanted to climb it. She wouldn't give up, she wanted to get to the top, always leading the way. She was so excited to get there, to climb to the highest point, to be in front, to get to the top first.

And she did.

APPENDIX

Dad's Story

As Ruth has visited different places and shared her story of Niki, I have sometimes been with her. At times, when the memories have evoked powerful emotions which have almost overwhelmed her, I have stepped in to share how dads are also affected by the death of a child.

Often when speaking of someone after their death, people are inclined to describe them in such glowing terms that you would think the person who has died was perfect in every way. I believe when I spoke at her farewell service I said that in no way could I say that Niki was an angel. Nevertheless, she was my "little princess" and when she died I felt that in some way I had failed her by not protecting her as a father should and blaming myself as a result. It is strange how irrational thoughts go around in your mind at times like that.

I grew up in South Devon at the end of World War Two, when the attitude of most people was that everyone just had to get on with life no matter how hard it was. It was a time when the British "stiff upper lip" was very prominent, summarised by the statement – "when things get tough, the tough get going!" I don't know whether my parents actually used these words but the message was very clear – "Big boys don't cry!" I therefore remember growing up learning not to show any emotions.

This suppression of my emotions was a very powerful factor with me, but following the death of Niki I realised that if I did not express my feelings and talk about Niki's death, then I would bottle them up, and this would cause real problems later in life. I remember standing in the shower one morning shouting at God with tears running down my cheeks, demanding he tell me why he had taken my daughter from me. If Jesus could cry then it was good enough for me. I believe that Christians must have a godly integrity to honestly face up to the reality of life, including the reality of pain. In a very calm voice (which, although not audible, was very real to me) I heard him say – "I have a job for her here in heaven looking after babies." When God speaks to you like that in such a very powerful way, there is nothing more you can say.

Nevertheless, sometime later I can remember reminding God that he promised to make all things work together for good to those who love him. This is a quote from the Bible[12] which has become the most important verse in my life. I told God that if he allowed such a terrible thing as the death of Niki to take place, then he was committed to doing something wonderful as a result. I am sure that God is quite happy for us to remind him about his promises as they are also an encouraging reminder to us as well.

Ruth has explained that denial is a strong factor at work in the early stages of the grief process. When we visited Whipsnade Zoo shortly after Niki died, I remember going into a café there and looking around to try and find a table with five seats. It took some time for me to adjust to there now only being four of us and I felt so stupid not realising that we were no longer a family of five.

This aspect of denial was to hit me particularly hard as I travelled into work via the underground service. Whenever I saw a little girl with an arm in plaster I thought it was Niki, or when a young child called out "daddy" I thought it was her calling for me. The day after Niki was buried I travelled into work and found myself in the same carriage as an old boss of mine. As usual, he asked how I was, and he got the "full story" which I think took him by surprise, but I had already determined not to supress my feelings.

The people at work were really wonderful and gave me as much time as I needed to get back to work. Nevertheless, the whole experience did affect my working situation. At this time, I was the Project Manager for London Operator Services and I had applied for a new post involving rolling out Total Quality Management across other parts of the London Telecommunications Service Organisation. I went for the interview, but had to explain the situation that following the death of Niki, I would not be able to spend vast amounts of time away from home during the week running training courses and conducting seminars. My priority at that time was to support Ruth, Steve, and Paul. Very reluctantly, they were therefore unable to offer me the post.

In particular, I needed to be very supportive to Ruth when she started to run The Compassionate Friends Group and was answering phone calls from distraught parents at all hours of the day or night. Dealing with bereaved parents was not something that I could see myself doing and when the group first met in our house I envisaged I would be a sort of butler, opening the door for people and making cups of tea or coffee. When so many people arrived, we could not accommodate them all in one room, and before I knew it I was with some of them in another room, sharing about heaven!

When Ruth started her pastoral care and Christian counselling training I suddenly realised that I was completely ill-prepared to counsel people, and in trying to help people I could be doing them more harm than good. I had previously been trained to be a counsellor at Billy Graham evangelistic rallies and was at that time an elder in my church. So, when I had the opportunity to take early retirement I applied to take a three-week residential course in Christian counselling. This experience was a life changer for me, but whilst attending the course I decided to return home at the weekends to be with Ruth and the boys, particularly as it was around the time of Niki's birthday.

This experience created in me a real desire to help people through some of their problems and, in particular to try and ensure the problems did not occur in the first place. There is a verse in the Bible which talks about us being able to comfort those in any trouble with the comfort we ourselves receive from God.[33] This was a particular example of how God started to work something good to come out of our experience. Over the following years, I started to counsel different people and organised training courses on various aspects of helping people. It was amazing to see that when the counselling requests reduced, the training courses increased and vice versa. Although after a few years we ceased doing formal counselling, we are continuing to use the same skills to come alongside and help people who seem to recognise that we have still got something to offer them.

During this time, I was approached by the local branch of Cruse Bereavement Care, where Ruth was a supervisor, to help develop their procedures and run the office for them. Again, this was something that I enjoyed doing, and from time to time I had to speak with bereaved people over the telephone. Often after spending time listening to people's stories, they would say what a wonderful help it had been to them and I was left thinking what on earth had I done apart from listening to them? This proves to me that anyone can be a great help to someone who is grieving by just listening to them tell their story.

Although I was unable to take up the earlier training job with British Telecom, I was now able to use and enjoy my gifting in other ways. Over the years, I have helped to develop a variety of training courses for local churches and other organisations on understanding and helping people. Sometimes Ruth has shared the teaching with me, but as this is not her gifting, I have enjoyed doing most of it myself. Recently I travelled to Uganda, and taught "helping people" skills to local pastors using similar material.

When someone dies, the loss affects people in different ways and one of the things that I lost with the death of Niki was the opportunity as a father to give my daughter away in marriage. This was a big loss for me and so it was a great privilege for me to be asked by Ruth's niece to give her away in marriage. Andrea was a small bridesmaid at our own wedding and over the years had started to call me "Poncle" – a mixture of pops and uncle. It was therefore a real joy to participate in her marriage ceremony in this way and to compensate in some small way for missing out on my own daughter's wedding.

Sometimes people have asked why this tragedy happened to us with the suggestion that we did not deserve it. This is not something that has ever crossed our minds, as we live in a fallen and broken world where bad things can happen to anyone. We are not particularly special people, and at times we have come alongside other families where a child has died, only for marriages, relationships, and families to be broken and destroyed by what has happened. In the Bible, the Apostle Paul wrote to one church, saying that he did not want them to grieve like the rest of mankind, who have no hope.[39] What makes grieving with hope different from grieving without hope is that hope gives us a glimpse of the eternal purposes of God and that something better is yet to come.

My experiences haven't turned me into an emotional sentimentalist. Ruth often reminds me that I am more of a thinker than a feeler, although I must confess that, over the years, I have become a "hugger!" Nevertheless, for both of us, what has happened to us has brought about a deeper maturity, compassion, and sensitivity for others. Others seem to recognise this in us and as a result are more willing to share with us. The desire of our hearts is to see people built up so that they become mature, attaining to the whole measure of the fullness of Christ, using the setbacks of life and changing them into stepping stones of maturity.

Epilogue To My Readers

If you've had a child that has died, or even some of you, devastatingly, more than one child that has died, my heart goes out to you. I care, so much. The pain is indescribable – part of you has been ripped out, torn away. My empathy, and the comfort of others, may help a little, but the only thing bigger than the terrible pain is God's indescribable love. He's the only one who can keep lifting your head above the water when it feels like you are drowning in your grief. I truly believe that he is the only reason I am what I am today, after such a tragedy, after feeling I could never be happy again, ever. He carried me through to a place where I could bear our loss, move forward, and live again. He waits to do the same for you, so I urge you to put yourself in his hands and trust him to carry you through.

If you knew Niki, or our family at the time, June 1987, I pray you can see now how it was that we were able to keep walking through the terrible dark valley of grief. Some of you thought we were strong people, with a strong faith in God. We weren't, and we aren't extraordinary people. We just have an extraordinary heavenly Father, and in our utter weakness we depended on *him* to carry us through. I hope you've seen, in my honest account, that this is not a way to escape pain in our lives. I don't promise that, but in the pain, God takes the weight, makes it bearable, and even brings joy back into our lives. We don't know what life will throw at us, but we know there will always be hard times, pain, sorrow, because this life, this world, is imperfect. But I also know, without a doubt, that knowing God as my Father means I am not alone – whatever lies ahead. He waits to make you his child too.

To all of you who are suffering loss and bereavement, I would say – allow yourselves to walk through the journey, it can't be rushed. Through the initial shock, numbness, denial, not believing it's true and never wanting to believe it's true; through anger, loss of confidence, anxiety about other possible losses and safety of loved ones; through blackness, depression, not wanting to wake up and live through another day, look for the help you need. Look out for the one or two who will walk alongside you without trying to make you better, who will listen well before giving advice. I pray you have such friends, who can bear to experience your pain with you and not try to cover it. These people are precious.

If you feel there is no one around you like that, then do turn to those organisations that can offer help, such as:

The Compassionate Friends. www.tcf.org.uk

Cruse Bereavement Care. www.cruse.org.uk

Survivors of Bereavement by Suicide. www.uk-sobs.org.uk

Stillbirth and Neonatal Death. www.uk-sands.org.uk

Sudden Infant Death Syndrome. www.sidsandkids.org/bereavement-support

And many more to be found online.

If you would like to contact me you are welcome to do so via the website: www.shewentahead.com

Notes

1. Psalm 62:5
2. Ephesians 4:14
3. Psalm 18:2,4,6
4. 1 Corinthians 10:13 (GNB)
5. Psalm 23:4
6. Psalm 84:5-7 (NLT)
7. Deuteronomy 33:27
8. Catherine Marshall, *To Live Again,* Fount Paperbacks/Collins
9. Isaiah 40:11(GNB)
10. Psalm 27:5
11. Psalm 27:13
12. Romans 8:28
13. Psalm 40:1-3
14. Isaiah 40:28
15. John 3:16
16. Hebrews 9:15
17. John 17:24 (NLT)
18. 1 Corinthians 2:9-10
19. 1 Corinthians 1:8,27
20. Psalm 62:1,2,8
21. Colossians 3:2
22. 1 Corinthians 15:13-14 (NLT)
23. 1 Corinthians 15:35 (NLT)
24. 1 Corinthians 15:44(NLT)
25. Psalm 18:9,11
26. Psalm 31:9,2-4
27. Isaiah 61:3
28. Psalm 91:1-4
29. Psalm 91:5
30. Psalm 91:14-15 (NLT)
31. Philippians 2:5
32. Philippians 2:17
33. 2 Corinthians 1:3,4
34. 2 Corinthians 1:9
35. 2 Corinthians 1:10
36. Psalm 103:4
37. Psalm 103:15-16
38. Micah 7:7
39. 1 Thessalonians 4:13

COSTLY WORSHIP

Mary, from Bethany, so loved Jesus
Her offering of worship was complete;
She broke her precious jar of perfume
And poured it all over his feet!

Some thought that was over indulgent,
One year's wages thrown away;
How they could have used that money,
But it all went to Jesus that day!

What an extravagant way to behave,
Giving her all, not just a part;
But how it delighted her Lord,
Receiving treasure from her heart.

Our lives are made like that -
Sealed pots - fragrant perfume within.
When a crack appears – how we fret,
Anxious to make it right again.

We don't realise that through that crack
Such sweet fragrance can waft out.
We're too busy trying to seal it,
Not seeing what it's all about.

But when nothing we do makes it better,
And it feels like we're falling apart;
Our lives are shattered – where's God?
I'm left with a broken heart.

I must get the pieces together,
Make my life as it was before.
Oh, which bit goes where? I'm confused,
I can't go on... any more.

Our Maker understands us best,
He knows what He's really about;
He filled us with his fragrance,
For the purpose of letting it out.

The pot lies in pieces, yes,
But the fragrance reaches above;
As we give ourselves into his hands
He breathes in our worship and love.

He knows how much it costs
To worship in the midst of pain;
He trod the path before us
And shares it with us, again.

He won't stick the bits back together,
He'll mould and shape anew;
In his hands we don't have to struggle,
So rest, and let God embrace **you**!

RG